ASTROLOGY *for* SUCCESS

Make the Most of
Your Sun Sign Potential

CASS & JANIE JACKSON

D1504297

HAMPTON ROADS

To David, Liz, Sue and Paul—
our family and our greatest success.

Cover and interior design by Kathryn Sky-Peck

Hampton Roads Publishing Company, Inc.
Charlottesville, VA 22906
Distributed by Red Wheel/Weiser, LLC
www.redwheelweiser.com

Sign up for our newsletter and special offers by going to
www.redwheelweiser.com/newsletter/

ISBN: 978-1-57174-794-5

Library of Congress Control Number: 2017958226

Printed in the United States of America
IBI

10 9 8 7 6 5 4 3 2 1

CONTENTS

ACKNOWLEDGMENTS

There is no way that we could acknowledge and thank all the people who have helped us to write this book. It is truly said, though, that the best way to learn a subject is to teach it.

That being said, we would like to thank all our students who, over the years, have asked us so many questions and thereby taught us so much.

INTRODUCTION

You may never have considered any possible connection between astrology and success, but you can start to think about it now. Even if you know nothing about astrology, you are almost certain to know your zodiac sign. You may also know, albeit vaguely, that each sign is defined by a number of positive and negative traits. It is these characteristics—which are your inborn strengths and weaknesses—that shape your life. In the twelve sections of this book you will find details of traits specific to each sign of the zodiac, together with suggestions on how best to use the positive aspects and modify the negative ones.

Success means different things to different people, but whatever it means to you, success is what you want from life. And you will not be happy if you are not getting it. Therefore, if you are dissatisfied with your present situation, it's time to make some changes. You are the only one who can do this. Nobody else can do it for you, nor can they decide on the path you need to follow. Ultimately, you are what you think you are. To paraphrase a well-known quotation: if you think you are a failure or if you think you are a success, you are probably right.

Your first decision is that you want to be successful, but your next step demands a little thought. What does success mean to you? It's essential to make up your mind about this before you start planning changes. If you do not have a clear idea of where you want to go, you are likely to drift around in circles, getting nowhere. Do not be influenced by the views of other people or by the generally accepted idea that success equates with wealth.

Once you have reached this all-important decision, you will need to work out how you are going to get what you want. You will find this book invaluable in making suggestions about the goals that are most suitable for you and methods for attaining them. You may wonder how this is possible, without the authors having personal knowledge of you and your life. The answer, as always, lies in the stars.

When you read the chapter about your personal zodiac sign, you will probably recognize yourself, warts and all. In order to get the maximum benefit from this book, some facts need to be faced—and they are not all pleasant. You may feel that we are overemphasizing your negative traits, but the point is that you should recognize them so that you can minimize them. Remember that you also have plenty of positive assets that will speed you on your way.

If you find that the details for your sign do not make a snug fit, read through the other sections in search of one that suits you better. Such a discrepancy could be due to the fact that your rising sign, your Moon sign, or some other feature in your chart modifies or even overpowers your Sun sign personality. For the same reason, you may find that methods advocated for other signs may appeal to you more than those suggested for your own. No problem. There is no need to stick with your own sign to the exclusion of all others. This book is designed to help you on the road to success, so take from it what you will.

Whichever star sign is yours and whatever inborn traits it may contain, there is one essential that you share with all other signs. You must take a positive approach to life. There is something almost magical about positive thought. Doors that you never knew existed can swing open. Opportunities you have never dreamed of present themselves. Other people become anxious to help you. The positive approach, allied to your own positive characteristics, can change your life, so make it happen.

So now you are ready to set off on your search for happiness and success. Take into consideration the suggestions that we make here and you cannot fail. Success is just around the corner—but it is up to you to find it. Reach for the stars!

Elements and Qualities

In this book, the section for each star sign of the zodiac begins by referring to elements and qualities. If you are new to astrology, you may find these terms confusing. Here is a brief explanation.

The zodiac is divided into twelve signs. Three of the signs are given to each element and there are four elements, each of which has its own attributes. The four elements are Fire, Earth, Air, and Water.

The Fire signs are Aries, Leo, and Sagittarius. These are the dynamic people of this world.

The Earth signs are Taurus, Virgo, and Capricorn. These are the planners of this world.

The Air signs are Gemini, Libra, and Aquarius. These are the bright intellectuals of this world.

The Water signs are Cancer, Scorpio, and Pisces. These are the artistic visionaries of this world.

Then there are the three qualities, the properties of which are given to four signs. The three qualities are Cardinal, Fixed, and Mutable.

The Cardinal signs are Aries, Cancer, Libra, and Capricorn. These are the assertive, enterprising types who get things off the ground and who can energize other people.

The Fixed signs are Taurus, Leo, Scorpio, and Aquarius. These are the determined types who make successful businesspeople.

The Mutable signs are Gemini, Virgo, Sagittarius, and Pisces. These are the adaptable types who adjust well to change.

As you will see from the table below, each sign shares an element with two others and a quality with three others, but no sign is exactly like any other.

Quality	Fire	Earth	Air	Water
Cardinal	Aries	Capricorn	Libra	Cancer
Fixed	Leo	Taurus	Aquarius	Scorpio
Mutable	Sagittarius	Virgo	Gemini	Pisces

ARIES

Main Characteristics

(Typically March 21 to April 19)

Aries is a cardinal fire sign. It is no coincidence that this is the first sign of the zodiac. Those born under this sign have no compunction about clambering over others to get to the front of the line—then they take charge of the situation. This is their way of life and the only one they understand. They were born to lead.

If you are a typically headstrong Aries, you will be convinced that you know best about everything. You will rush enthusiastically into a new venture, but if you encounter problems, you will quietly forget the idea. If you learn some self-discipline, it will prevent you from abandoning a project simply because your enthusiasm wanes. Aries should never embark on an enterprise that requires a steady, plodding approach because you are a sprinter rather than a long distance runner.

Your pioneering, competitive Aries spirit means that you are likely to succeed when self-employed. This suits your temperament, allowing you to make your own decisions and to exploit your dynamism to the full. Self-employment also allows you to make maximum use of another Aries strength: your ability to concentrate totally on the matter in hand. Let others run around in circles; your single-mindedness is an invaluable asset that can greatly assist your quest for success. Aries also does well when working in large organizations, especially those with a definite structure to them, such as the police, the armed services, and in teaching.

Often, your physical characteristics mirror your Aries temperament. You are probably tall, lean, and bold looking. You hold your head high; ready to take on all comers. Your firm Aries handshake typifies your strength and integrity.

The clothes you wear often reflect your personality as they are the best that you can afford. Some Aries are real clotheshorses, others lean more toward practicality, but you like to be appropriately dressed at all times—and you probably have a marked fondness for all shades of red.

THE ARIES PLAN FOR SUCCESS

Where are you now?

Take some time to think about this. Wherever you are now is the place from which you will have to start on your journey toward success. Do you feel that you are getting nowhere and drifting along aimlessly? If you answer yes to this question, decide what you are going to do about it.

New Beginnings

Your quest for success is an opportunity to make a completely fresh start. Consider what you want out of life. What changes—and even sacrifices—are you willing to make in pursuit of your goal?

Now is the time to consider the initial stages of your new development, so list the areas in your life that you will need to alter on your way to success. Use one page for each area of your life and title it with the change that you want to make. For example, you may know that you become irritated when you are kept waiting—for anything.

Under each heading, write precisely how you want to change. Then detail a plan that will enable you to implement that one change. Some changes may take longer to implement than others—allow for this in your planning.

By the time you have finished listing the alterations you want to make, you will probably have quite a sheaf of pages. Now place them in order of your own personal priority.

Write today's date at the top of the first page, tomorrow's date on the second page, and so on.

Page one is your Plan for Today. Act on it immediately. Don't procrastinate. Do it now. There is another task to be done tomorrow. If you truly want success you will not cheat and skip any of these vital steps. You listed them because you recognized their importance. There was no compulsion. If you cheat, you are only fooling yourself.

Conscientiously repeat this process, making one change every day. At the same time, maintain and build on those you have made previously. Review your list frequently to reinforce your motivation. You may have to repeat this process several times, but stick with it.

Your Principles for Success

Success comes for Aries if they make the most of their positive traits and suppress their negative qualities. This requires action. Start right NOW.

Dispense with negative thoughts about yourself, your job, or your aims in life. Fix your sights on the stars, not in the gutter. Give your all to the job in hand but try always to have some new scheme at the back of your mind as something to which you can look forward.

See yourself as a winner and keep that image burning bright. If you do hit a losing streak, maintain a positive attitude. It's strange but true that if you expect and demand success, you will get it.

Remember that you are an Aries; therefore, you are in charge of your own destiny.

Try to move in successful social circles. Make friends with positive people who will encourage you and avoid negative types who will drag you down. Always be pleasant and courteous, because one day you may need to ask a favor of your former boss or your neighbor. Success is not a goal to be reached; it is a lifelong journey, one that involves other people, no matter how independent you are.

▶ Set Goals

Your motivation will be enhanced if you set specific goals. What do you want to achieve? What does success mean to you? In what areas of your life do you want to succeed? Before you start making plans, it is essential that you know exactly where you want to go. If you set off on a long journey without a map, you will almost certainly lose your way and may never reach your destination. There is no better way to keep motivated than to find a guide. Someone who has already walked the same path can offer invaluable support. He will have the experience of the right way to go, the shortcuts you can take and the pitfalls to avoid. Choose your mentor carefully and beware of false gurus. Find out how successful your "expert" is before accepting his words of wisdom.

To maintain your enthusiasm you will have to remain flexible. However carefully you plan, life may attempt to trip you up. This is a common experience, so don't throw an Aries temper tantrum. Consider the situation carefully and see what you can learn from it.

▶ Where to Start

Aries is a natural leader. Don't let this go to your head and try not to force your opinions on others, even when you are convinced (as you usually are) that you know best. Cope with less forceful characters by employing diplomacy and tact. This will not come easily to you, but you must remember that nobody likes to be pushed around. Lead by example. Your superiority will soon be recognized and everybody will be happy. The followers of this world will see you as someone who can free them from the responsibility of leadership.

Aries never suffers fools gladly, but your natural impatience can be a useful tool. You are the one whose enthusiasm will inspire your team to forge ahead and get the job done. Try to curb your intolerance when others cannot keep up with you.

There are times when you become exasperated with yourself. This makes you difficult to live with until the situation is resolved. It is this self-impatience that makes you abandon a half-finished job. Resist the temptation to quit, because stick-to-itiveness pays dividends. This is the time when you need to call upon your Aries adaptability. Almost invariably there is more than one way of solving a problem, so instead of giving up in a huff, set your mind on finding a way around the difficulty.

Make the most of your second-greatest Aries asset—your ability to concentrate totally on the matter in hand. Let others run around in circles. Remain immersed in your thoughts until you come up with the solution to the current problem. Your colleagues will recognize you as a deep thinker and respect you for it.

▶ Your Plan of Action

NOW is the time to start fresh projects and launch new ideas. Aries subjects are brimming over with inborn energetic talent, so make the most of yours. Seize the initiative whenever you can and let others follow like sheep. You are a Ram—the one who leads.

Competition brings out the best in you—but do not confuse competitiveness with aggression. Accept with good grace that other people's ideas may be better than yours. Then learn what you can from their success and try again another day. You may eventually find that you have built a bigger and better mousetrap.

You are certainly a talker rather than a listener. In fairness, what you have to say is usually worth hearing. Even so—learn how to listen. This way you will gain knowledge from the successful people you meet. Don't be afraid of failure. Have a go. If you do not, you will never know whether or not your idea or project would have been successful. If you fail, learn from your mistakes and resolve not to repeat them.

▶ Getting It All in Focus

For most Aries, success equates with prosperity and the financial area is usually the first one you will think of. Money management may present some problems for you, particularly when success comes suddenly.

Organize your financial affairs and put aside what you will need for your essential outgoings. If there is any money left, spend as much of it as you like. If there isn't anything left to spend, then so be it—at least you are solvent. Solvency is particularly important to Aries. How will you finance your next project without money?

Most Aries have a tendency to rush into making decisions about important matters that deserve more thought. You are confident that you will be able to jump any hurdles that arise, and you cannot believe that there may be a fence just around the corner that is too high for even you to leap. The result? Chaos.

Careful consideration of all the details of every aspect of a project is alien to Aries, but it is time well spent. Don't agree with a suggestion simply because it has instant appeal. For once in your life, think carefully. Until you are sure the idea is right for you (and for the other people in your life) resist the temptation to leap into something new. You may be willing to live on stale bread in a hovel until your dream comes true but your wife and family may not be so keen. Above all, dismiss any suggestion that you may be missing out on "a chance in a million." So far as Aries is concerned, this is extremely unlikely. You know a good deal when you see one.

Money and Your Career

You love to spend money and you cannot resist buying clothes. Male Ariens will always have the best car that you can get for your money. No Arien likes to have empty pockets. Some of you are generous to your families, others are not—but you are unlikely to be open handed to outsiders. Either way, it is just as well that you are ambitious, because you need a high income so that you can have the money you need.

Times of Change

There are times in your life when certain planets return to the position in the sky that they occupied when you were born. It is at the times of those returns that you will consider the need for change. The two returns that will influence success in your life are the first Saturn return when you are about 30 years of age, and the Uranus half-return when you are about 40.

Age 25–35

For Aries, the first Saturn return is a time when you will gladly put formal education behind you to look around for those areas in which you can be successful. It is time to stop being the manic mountain climber. You need to settle down, without losing your Aries enthusiasm for life. During this period, you will learn to curb your "I know best" attitude by substituting a little patience.

Age 36–39

The Uranus half-return marks the stage in your life when you may realize that, as far as success is concerned, you have been barking up the wrong tree. Your true Aries personality comes to the fore now when, without batting an eyelid, you can change your whole life-career, partner, beliefs and/or interests. Hopefully, you will have learned by now that patience is indeed a virtue.

Age 57–60

The second Saturn return brings yet another change. If you have been following a typically Arien career, it will now be too active for you. Why not retire and look for something easier that will take you through to your real retirement?

Career Possibilities

1. Politician
2. Trade union leader
3. Teacher
4. Soldier
5. Pilot
6. Air/sea rescuer
7. Police officer
8. Fire fighter
9. Engineer
10. Motor mechanic
11. Electrician
12. Office manager
13. Secretary
14. Sports person
15. Athlete
16. Gym trainer
17. Scout leader
18. Psychic medium

▶ *Do What You Love Doing*

Success in life usually comes from doing what you most like to do. You are the only person who knows what that is. Aries always needs a challenging job that provides plenty of action. You must be allowed to think on your feet and come up with new ideas.

You're clever with your hands and would make a superb motor mechanic or electronics engineer. Your enthusiasm makes you a successful sales rep. Your physical energy and your need to be in charge make you the ideal person to run a gym or health club. In fact, you will excel in any trade or profession where the results depend solely on your own hard work. The one thing Aries cannot endure is sitting at a desk every day in a routine office job.

You will blossom in most creative fields, like painting, music, and writing, where you can work alone. You have great communication skills and will do well in journalism, public relations, advertising, radio, television, or the theater.

Despite your lack of tact and diplomacy, a political career may appeal to you. A surprising number of Aries become politicians. Always reaching for the moon, they set their sights on the White House or 10 Downing Street—and some of them have made it, so why not you?

In business, Aries make first-rate chief executives but find minor positions well-nigh impossible to handle. You need to be "top dog" and are always convinced that your ideas are superior to any others. (They usually are.)

Providing the project is one that holds your interest and enthusiasm, you can succeed in just about any field you fancy. Aries can start out running a small corner shop and end up heading a multinational organization. Thanks to your energy and ambition, the sky is the limit.

Aries Health

If you want to be successful, you must look after your health. As an Aries, this means looking after your head. You come into the world headfirst and lead with your head for the rest of your life. This leaves the Ram open to quite a few ailments.

Headaches will almost certainly be your biggest health problem, ranging from frequent minor niggles to full-scale migraine attacks. These can be caused by or result in stress. All too often this, linked with your strong Aries energy, produces fireworks. As you well know, a volatile Aries is not to be tangled with lightly.

However, have the sense to realize that an endless circle of stress—headaches—stress is not going to help you on your road to success.

Your passion for exercise will help to keep you on an even keel—but do not be tempted into an excess of physical activity. Though you will hate to admit it, even Aries gets older as the years pass. Regular exercise is essential to your health, but do not overdo it.

Periods of relaxation will help with your headaches, irritability, stress, and fiery nature. Relaxation is alien to Aries, but you should try to master it. If you do not, you are on the road to self-destruction, continuing on your headstrong way until a nervous breakdown results. What price success then?

Aries Relationships

Family ties are important to Aries, and you will not consider yourself successful unless you are on excellent terms with your partner, parents, siblings, and your own children.

You are usually drawn to other Fire signs—Leo and Sagittarius. A business partnership with Leo will be strong and long-lasting. You will probably have disagreements but they will be short-lived. Basically, you will both be aiming for the same goal and this fact will overcome any problems.

In your private life, your Leo partner will not give you an easy ride. You are two passionate people and both enjoy having things your own way. This will make for a turbulent relationship, but your arguments will not last long. You will both want to kiss and make up. This partnership strengthens as time passes and it is likely to last a lifetime. Both signs are attractive to the opposite sex, so beware of jealousy.

In business or in love, a partnership with Leo or Sagittarius is likely to be beneficial to you both. The fiery Aries personality ensures strong, if somewhat stormy relationships, particularly if you can manage to control your selfish streak.

There is another combination that often works even better than the fire sign group for you, and that is to team up with someone born under one of the air signs of Gemini, Libra, and Aquarius. Their logical minds slow your headlong rushes and encourage you to stop and think from time to time. They are cooler, less likely to explode in rage or to become jealous of you, so this fire/air combination often serves you well.

Aries Positive and Negative Traits

Your search for success should be geared to your own personality, strengths, and weaknesses. Check out the following list of Aries positive and negative traits. Mark those that apply to you. Now start accentuating the positive and eliminating the negative.

Positive traits	Negative traits
Adaptable	Arrogant
Enthusiastic	Assertive
Confident	Easily bored
Courageous	Impatient
Creative	Combative
Dexterous	Domineering
Energetic	Impulsive
Enterprising	Irritable
Hard-working	Intolerant
Independent	Jealous
Born leader	Naive
Multitalented	Quick-tempered
Politically adroit	Selfish
Born teacher	Demanding

Over to You

If you did not have a driving ambition to be successful, you would not be reading this book. Consider this an omen showing that this is the time to begin a new phase in your life. This book offers ideas about how you can achieve success. Put these ideas into action and you will never look back.

Always remember that Aries is the leader. Expect others to follow, and they probably will. Forget about any chances you may have missed in the past. Devise your plan of action and go for it NOW.

2

TAURUS

Main Characteristics

(Typically April 20 to May 20)

Taurus is a fixed earth sign and these two properties sum you up completely. Fixed earth is exactly as it sounds—strong and unyielding. You are extremely conscientious about any responsibilities you undertake and you have a patient and logical approach to any problem. Tenacity is your middle name. Not given to snap decisions, you take your time about everything, but once you have decided on a course of action, you will not budge. Others can forget about a debate on the pros and cons of a case because you have made up your mind.

Not everyone will appreciate these qualities. Some will see you as decidedly inflexible. It must also be admitted that on occasion, you can exhibit a truly bullish rage. You dislike change and prefer to stick with well-tested methods. Originality is not one of your talents. Neither is sparkling conversation, because you can be ill at ease with strangers. Sometimes you try to cover this up with heavy-handed attempts at humor, so your best bet is to admit that you can be shy at times and to allow others to do the talking.

You have a loyal and loving disposition. Only your immediate family will be aware of your sensuality and artistic leanings. They also appreciate your caring nature, your reliability, and your self-control in a crisis. You are a true family person and it would take a lot for you to walk out on your loved ones.

Your most striking physical features are your good complexion and your hair. Many women born under this sign also have beautiful "bovine" eyes. Weight may be a problem for you, as you tend to be chubby, so plenty of exercise and strict dieting may be the only answer. Though you love soft and delicate fashions, you normally wear comfortable clothes in which you can feel relaxed.

THE TAURUS PLAN FOR SUCCESS

Where are you now?

Like most people, Taurus dreams of success—though you are usually not very sure what you mean by that word. Fortunately, you are not an impulsive type. You may feel eager to get going, but first you must understand where you are right now. Only after careful assessment of your present position can you decide whether you really want to forge ahead in search of new pastures.

Taurus hates change. If you strike out in a new direction, you may have to reinvent yourself. Are you prepared to do that? Consider carefully. You may even decide that you are quite comfortable with your present way of life.

New Beginnings

In your search for success, you will need to make the most of your positive attributes. You will also have to learn how to deal with what appear to be your negative characteristics. Believe it or not, these can be your strongest allies, if they are channeled correctly. Your stubborn nature will ensure that you see projects through to a successful conclusion. You will never be a source of brilliant off-the-cuff suggestions, because you think things through carefully and you refuse to be hurried. When you do reach a decision, it's usually a sensible one—and nobody is going to change it.

Your enduring patience can be the key to your career. Your tolerance, persistence and the urge to help others will stand you in good stead. It is your destiny to care for others.

Taurus enjoys the security of a set routine. However, do not close your mind to modern methods because they can be easier and more efficient than the old ways. Give new suggestions your full attention and consider trying them out.

Undoubtedly, your family will see you as a dependable provider. This is largely due to the Taurus dislike of unpredictability. It's essential that you avoid any career that lacks a regular, steady income, so working on commission is not for you.

By nature you are a placid sort of person, but do try to exercise regularly. Not only will it do your physique a power of good, it will also improve the circulation of blood to your brain and make you feel more awake and aware.

Your Principles for Success

If you are looking for a new career, seek a situation where your practical and capable quality will be needed. Aim for a well-established business where you will be working with congenial colleagues. Avoid negative people at all costs. They will undermine your self-confidence and optimism.

It's not possible to please all the people all the time, so do not even try. If you are convinced that you are acting wisely, ignore what others say and go ahead with your usual quiet determination. Undoubtedly, you will have to face some criticism. Taurus can be deeply hurt by this, but refuse to deviate from your chosen path.

Liking a set routine can be a valuable part of your career plan. Before taking any action at all, work out your success strategy. Tailor it precisely to your own strengths and weaknesses, likes and dislikes. This method will provide you with the security so essential to Taurus.

However happy you feel now, don't become a stick in the mud. We all change with time, often without realizing it. Reexamine your goals. Do they still excite you? If not, it is time to consider changes.

Consider carefully—exactly what does success mean for you? You are not the sort of person to be concerned with status. Your main drive is for security. For this reason, you set great store by possessions. It follows that having more worldly goods may mean success to you. You like comfort and pleasure. To what lengths will you go to obtain them? Your ultimate success may depend on getting this right. Mull this over in true Taurus fashion. Nevertheless, do not forget that if you are to reach your goal, a decision must be made. You cannot procrastinate forever.

▶ Set Goals

Generally speaking, Taurus is neither academic nor interested in paperwork. The fact remains that the most satisfactory way to plan your future is to get your thoughts on paper. Write down your goals and hopes. Give yourself deadlines. You will be surprised how much more real your plans appear when you see them in black and white.

It is worthwhile to set aside some time for this project. Once you have created this blueprint for your future, you will have no further doubts about your ultimate destination and how you are going to reach it. You may like to carry this plan with you in a notebook that you can refer to from time to time. Taurus often needs reassurance, and these notes will show that you are still on the right road. They will motivate you if your enthusiasm starts to flag. Moreover, if you do make mistakes, a written plan will swiftly set you back on course.

Another benefit to be gained from creating your blueprint is psychological. By writing down your plans you are making a statement of intent, changing your wishes into goals. You have made a commitment by putting these plans on paper. You know beyond all possible doubt where you are going and how to get there.

These plans will also help you to develop a genuine passion for whatever it is that you want from life. This is the difference between a goal and a wish. Passion puts action into your plans and intentions. Despite your quiet exterior, Taurus has a deeply passionate nature. Use it to the full in your search for success.

It is scarcely necessary to advise you, of all people, to ensure that your plans and deadlines are feasible. Check everything through. Then go ahead with confidence. If you are to achieve the success you seek, you will have to learn to adapt yourself to the world as it is—not as you would like it to be. You do not like being hassled or hurried. That is fair enough, very few of us do. The fact remains that the pace of life is increasing and, if you are to succeed, you must learn to cope with it. Try to go with the flow.

This need for speeding up will not be welcomed by Taurus, but do not let it rattle you. Do your best and—as always—refuse to be rushed into snap decisions. When you know that a decision needs to be made, think about it well beforehand so that you have time for your own deliberations. Why not make a list of pros and cons? Above all, keep your head.

▶ *Where to Start*

Once you decide to take a different path in life, change will be inevitable. This has been mentioned earlier, but there is another aspect of this decision that you should consider carefully. Change will affect not only you; it will also affect your nearest and dearest. This is one time when you should not keep your plans to yourself. Tell your family about your ideas. If, in your usual reserved fashion, you say nothing until you present them with a *fait accompli*, they will be hurt and resentful. Let them feel part of your plan. Invite their suggestions—but never forget that the final decision must be yours. One of your greatest assets is that you are prepared to work hard to achieve your goals. This is an excellent start on your road to success.

It is essential for Taurus to have a sense of stability and you do worry—often unnecessarily—about money. Your anxieties could well hinder your chances of succeeding. In fact, they could even prevent you from getting your success strategy off the ground. So one of the

first things you must do is to lighten up. Easier said than done? Yes—
but think carefully. Has your habit of worrying ever—even once—
altered the outcome of any situation? Stop worrying—right now.

▶ Your Plan of Action

Once you have committed yourself to a plan of action, go one step
further and resolve to look for better ways of doing things. New
ways may be better ways. It is up to you to find out. This does
not mean that you need to enroll in umpteen courses in esoteric
subjects. It is unlikely that you will need to develop new talents.
Rather you should concentrate on developing the skills you already
have—and this could well mean updating your knowledge.

This drive for improvement need not be confined to your business affairs. It is all too easy for Taurus to sink happily into a rut. Have
a good look at your personal relationships, your home, your appearance—all aspects of your life—and see if they need polishing up.

Few can match the Taurus capacity for patience, which can be a
tremendous asset. You are not the type to quit, because you do not
achieve overnight success. When you are confident that you are on
the right path, you will keep doggedly on until you reach your target.

Because of your somewhat inarticulate nature, you find it difficult
to ask for advice. Try to overcome this. It is important that you keep on
learning—from business acquaintances, from your family and friends,
even from your competitors. Don't be too shy to say thank you when
you receive the help or advice you need. You will learn more about life
from other people than you will from a thousand books.

▶ Getting It All in Focus

In your chosen career path you will need organization, a structured
schedule, and financial security. These are essential to your nature.
Find a line of business that allows you to plan ahead. Not knowing
what to expect from day to day is a sure recipe for stress. Taurus cannot cope with uncertainty. You need the stability of a regular routine.
Without it, you are unlikely to achieve the goals you have in mind.

Those born under the sign of Taurus are among the financial wizards of the zodiac. Account books and balance sheets hold no terrors for you. Your almost instinctive grasp of sound financial management will provide a firm foundation for any business venture you undertake.

A typically Taurean weakness is a tendency to be a workaholic. Enthusiasm for your work is fine, but do not go over the top. It is not good for your health—and is even worse for your family. Schedule some regular "quality time" together and set aside some money purely for pleasure. Indulge yourself (and others) in the sort of superb meals you so much enjoy, or arrange a weekend break at a country hotel. The resulting relaxation is as good as money in the bank.

Money and Your Career

Security is the name of the game as far as your finances are concerned, so you prefer a job that offers a regular income that you can depend upon. You may not look for an exciting job but for one that pays reasonably well and that offers you a pension at the end of it. You are careful with money, but you will always spend it on your home, your family, and on a really good vacation.

Times of Change

There are times in your life when certain planets return to the position in the sky that they occupied when you were born. It is at the times of those returns that you will consider the need for change. The two returns that will influence success in your life are the first Saturn return when you are about 30 years of age, and the Uranus half-return when you are about 40.

Age 25–35

We are assured that life begins at 40, but for Taurus, changes are likely to appear a decade earlier. As you approach the age of 30 you may start feeling dissatisfied with your life and what you have achieved so far. This Saturn return is giving you the chance to make a fresh start. Guard against giving in to your obstinate Taurus streak. Success and happiness are just around the corner if you have the courage to reach out for them.

Age 36–39

If you went ahead and made changes near your 30th birthday, you should be reaping the benefits by the time of the Uranus half-return. Chances are that you are settling happily into your middle years, with no urge to change your current situation. However, do not panic if change is forced upon you. Your inborn persistence and placid nature will overcome all obstacles.

Age 57–60

You are quite likely to retire from the job that you have done for so many years at this age. If you have money, you can be happy puttering around at home and visiting friends, but if you need something extra, you will look around for a part-time occupation that has a creative element to it.

Career Possibilities

1. Builder
2. Garden designer
3. Farmer
4. Market gardener
5. Greengrocer
6. Caterer
7. Estate manager
8. Factory manager
9. Beautician
10. Hair and nail artist
11. Makeup artist
12. Massage therapist

13. Banker
14. Financial advisor
15. Accountant
16. Singer
17. Dancer
18. Actor

▶ Do What You Love Doing

Work surroundings are of primary importance to Taurus. A noisy workshop or the constant hubbub of a hotel kitchen is not for you. You prefer the calm ambience of a business office or the silence of a library. A traveling job is definitely not for you. Your environment needs to be set within the parameters of a reputable, stable, time-honored business. Let others dismiss this as dull. Security is all-important to you and vital to your success.

Banking or insurance would be a suitable profession for you. It will even make the best possible use of that sublime patience of yours. The only problem is that nowadays these jobs are sales oriented and everybody in them is encouraged to sell something at every opportunity. You cannot do this, so you have to ensure that your duties are as far from the public and the selling end of the business as possible.

Most Taurus subjects love the country and an outdoor life. Consider farming or floristry. Both careers demand patience. You cannot hurry the crops or the flowers. Others gravitate to the building trades where the combination of creating something useful, working with the hands, and being outdoors suits your temperament very well.

Your compassionate nature may lead you into one of the caring professions. You have the patience to care for elderly people, and you have a real affinity for animals. Working in the fields of architecture or interior design will allow you to express your artistic leanings. In fact, you could be successful in any one of a wide variety of careers. Just bear in mind that you must have stability and security and that your working environment is of primary importance.

Many Taureans can be found in the makeup departments of television and film studios; all three of the hairdressers in our local salon are of this sign. This is where your natural affinity for beauty and for working with your hands comes into play.

Taurus Health

Taurus subjects enjoy their food. You need to learn early in life that overeating leads to weight problems. This tendency increases as you get older, because you become less active and burn off fewer calories. Don't allow weight gain to get out of hand. It could lead to a number of other ailments that could adversely affect your working life.

The real Taurus problem area is usually the throat and neck region. You will almost certainly be more prone than most people to sore throats and neck ache. If you are a teacher or in any other position that over-uses the voice, then tonsillitis or laryngitis may crop up. Try singing in the shower, as it is an excellent antidote for stress and for throat problems.

Taurus usually has an extremely strong constitution and few health problems.

Taurus Relationships

Taurus can be a somewhat demanding partner, both in business and in private life. Virgo or Capricorn, which are also earth signs, could be your perfect lover and companion. There will be an instinctive understanding between you—and your warmth and passion will be equally matched. Like Taurus, both Virgo and Capricorn enjoy a quiet, gentle lifestyle and tend to prefer an evening at home.

If, on the other hand you are looking for real romance, you will find Cancer a sensitive partner—who will, like you, love good food. The Taurus might also find their ideal match in a Libra. Libras will be casual and easy going, give their undivided attention, and enjoy being entertained in romantic settings.

Look for a Virgo to be your business partner. A Virgo will not only complement your own talents, but may not be averse to occasionally acting in a supporting role. This could be a highly successful partnership. Just remember to be scrupulously honest with your partner and learn to cope with his sometimes blunt remarks.

Taurus Positive and Negative Traits

Take your first step toward success right now. Check out the following list of Taurus positive and negative traits. Mark those that apply to you. Now start accentuating the positive and eliminating the negative.

Positive traits	Negative traits
Affectionate	Boring
Artistic	Complacent
Dependable	Hedonistic
Domesticated	Inflexible
Gentle	Insensitive
Industrious	Jealous
Loving	Moody
Loyal	Materialistic
Placid	Obstinate
Practical	Possessive
Resourceful	Prejudiced
Sensuous	Resentful
Sensible	Self-pitying
Trustworthy	Stubborn

Over to You

This book is designed to help you decide what you most want out of life and to guide you on your way. First, though, you must heave yourself out of the rut you have occupied for so long. Only you can do that—so get moving. Look for new horizons and be prepared to accept change. At the same time, realize that Taurus always needs encouragement and support. Don't be reluctant to ask for help. Above all, do not forget that blueprint for success. Study it. Act on it. In addition, remember that NOW is the only time we have.

3

GEMINI

Main Characteristics

(Typically May 21 to June 21)

Gemini is a mutable air sign. This means you will easily adjust to your immediate surroundings—a valuable attribute in these days of rapid change. If you are unhappy with your environment, you will put up with it—but set about making subtle changes more to your liking. You are quick-witted and much more perceptive than the casual observer imagines. You watch and listen, then reach your own conclusions, often abandoning recognized theories. If anything puzzles you, you do not hesitate to ask for explanations.

Communication of all kinds is of primary importance to you, and you are never at a loss for words. Coupled with your love of gadgets, this makes you a natural computer whiz kid. Email, chat rooms, bulletin boards, and so forth were made for you, allowing you to satisfy your urge to communicate without leaving your workstation. Even minus your beloved computer, you would still contact others through the written word or—as you do now—by spending hours gossiping on the telephone. As an expansive and outgoing Gemini you find it easy to talk your way into or out of any situation.

Others see you as friendly, original, and amusing but rather superficial and elusive. Just when they think they are getting to know you and want you around, you disappear. The zodiac symbol for Gemini is the twins, which makes you something of a dual personality. You cannot stick around with one project, friend, or idea for long. Instead you are forever pursuing several lines of thought and action. Variety and change are essential to you. Even if you became rich or reached retirement age, you would still go out to work. You enjoy being involved in the outside world, keeping up to date, and being among people, so sitting around at home or spending your time in front of the television is not for you.

Those born under the sign of Gemini are usually tall, slim, and agile with a youthful complexion. You are likely to look younger than your years. Comfortable clothes that will not cramp your agility suit you best. Simple styles and bright colors like red, white, and yellow will accentuate your youthfulness.

THE GEMINI PLAN FOR SUCCESS

Where are you now?

As a Gemini, your primary need is to become more focused. Convinced that you have an unerring eye for the main chance, you are inclined to jump at the first opportunity. Be careful. You could jump out of the frying pan into the fire.

New Beginnings

Boring as it may seem, success for Gemini often depends on settling down. You need to forget the get-rich-quick schemes because they never work, and you should do some deep thinking about your future. Consider carefully your likes and dislikes. For example, you do not like hard manual labor, routine work, or regular hours. You prefer flexible organizations, diverse types of work, and frequent face-to-face contact with your colleagues. You must be honest with yourself. Stay away from your Gemini dream world and consider your many talents. Being financially clever gives you a head start. You are also good at wheeling and dealing. Thanks to your communicative skills you are an excellent teacher. Linguistic ability, too, often comes easily to Gemini.

These are just a few typical Gemini attributes. Ask a long-standing friend to help you add to the list. Often others know us better than we know ourselves. Then make two lists—things you do well and things you like to do. Now combine them into as many permutations as possible. Give this some serious thought and eventually you will come up with a combination that shouts, "YES!" For example, your skill at wheeling and dealing, money management, and communication may point you toward a financial career. Add your gift for languages and you could go even further.

Focus on your long-term future, rather than on the present and what is currently within easy grasp. Look for some line of business that offers the versatility you require.

Don't be tempted to alter everything. Changes may be necessary in certain aspects of your life, but you do not have to completely reinvent yourself. Build on the good things you already have.

Your Principles for Success

You, above all others, need to devise a clear strategy for success. This can present problems for inconsistent Gemini. Being single-minded seems contrary to your nature and—let's be honest—you often lack perseverance. Ensure that these weaknesses do not prevent you from starting on the road to success.

Don't even try to tell yourself that you are going to follow all the advice in this book. Just make up your mind that you will try, and ignore that inner voice urging you not to bother. Don't say you are going to start later, tomorrow, or next week. START NOW.

Nothing worth having comes easily, so accept that you are in for some hard work. Realize, too, that this means focused hard work, not jumping from one task to another. In this context, we are not just talking career. This need for focused effort applies to your private life as well. If you want a stable relationship, you have to work at it—you cannot be a flirt all your life. Again, you have to learn to be single-minded. There is no option.

It is essential for you to create a sound financial structure for both your family and your business life. On a day-to-day basis, you are good with money. However, if you are looking for a new beginning, you must make a long-term financial forecast. It's much the same as presenting a business plan to your bank when applying for a loan. This long-term forecast will free you from financial problems in the future, so that you can concentrate on more mundane matters.

▶ Set Goals

All the personal development "How To" books advise you to follow the example of the great achievers and set goals for your future. Here are six steps that will help you to do this.

1. List your goals. Cast your net wide and make the list as varied as possible. Include every aspect of your life in which you are seeking success—partnerships, family, friends, career, social activities, community work, and so on.

2. Revise the list placing the goals in order of importance. This can be difficult for Gemini, so do not rush the process.

3. Now create a list of tasks to be done in order to meet your goals. Some of your aims may take longer to achieve than others. List the steps to be taken for each goal.

4. Put a time factor on each of the tasks. Set a deadline for the completion of each one, but do not try to achieve the impossible. Allow the time to carry out each step correctly; avoid the Gemini tendency to flit from one thing to another.

5. Make a habit of reviewing the list each day. Measure your progress against it and tick off your successes. This will encourage

and can help to keep you in line. Accept that you may have to change your goals and tasks to suit changed circumstances—but beware of altering things just because you are bored.

6. Rejoice in your successes, but do not castigate yourself for your failures. Examine them to discover where you went wrong so that you will not make the same mistake again.

▶ *Where to Start*

In order to achieve success, you will have to take positive steps toward your goals. You will also need to eliminate your negative attributes. Obviously, the first step in this process is to recognize what they are. It is highly probable that you will not be able to do this without help. Gemini is not given to introspection, but now is the time to consider a few ideas about your personality.

Do you see yourself as a jack-of-all-trades and master of none? This is a common Gemini weakness. You hop, skip, and jump from one activity to another, gathering useless information as you go. As a result, a lot of people do not take you seriously, especially when you are in the throes of some new excitement. Your first priority is to change this negative trait into a positive one, so that your versatility is appreciated and used purposefully.

▶ *Your Plan of Action*

The Gemini tendency to flit from one interest to another can be extremely dangerous. No matter what project you are involved in, you often deviate into enticing new pathways. If you give in to this temptation, you are likely to find yourself involved in a project entirely different from the one on which you started. The solution lies in seeking out the shortest, straightest route to the goal you have in mind. Refuse to be lured into new pastures, and determine to keep your feet firmly on your original path. This is why it is vital for you to choose a goal that you are utterly convinced is totally right for you. You might decide on having two part-time jobs rather than one full-time one and thus bring much-needed variety into your life.

Having reached that first decision, try to become completely involved in reaching your goal. You can do this only if you enjoy your work. Gemini needs to work in seclusion, to guard against the siren call of new ideas. However, you also need contact with other people, so try to strike a happy medium. Discuss your work with your colleagues, but do not allow them to divert your attention from the job at hand.

Do not be afraid to put yourself first when and where it is necessary. Look upon your present mission as being all-important. You will almost certainly need to reorganize your life around this new undertaking. Decide what unnecessary obstructions can be stripped away to leave you a clear path to your goal.

▶ Getting It All in Focus

Once you have embarked on your new way of life—aiming for success—have confidence in your abilities. Tell others what you are doing. Ask for the support of your work mates and your partner. Be prepared for hardships and stumbling blocks, but expect to overcome them. Don't opt out at the first problem. Convert that conviction and hope into faith, which can be defined as a firm belief without logical proof. There is a theory that we create our own reality. Whether you accept that or not does not matter. However, it is a fact that if you believe in your eventual success, you are far more likely to reach your goals.

Avoid all forms of self-deception. Reinventing yourself is one thing; being deceitful is something else. Take pride in being totally honest—with yourself and with others. Being caught out in one small act of deception can ruin your chances of success forever. Don't take the risk. Self-deception is the worst form of duplicity. Those who practice it eventually believe their own lies until they reach their inevitable comeuppance and downfall.

Remember that your success or failure is likely to depend not only on your own efforts, but also on a number of other people. No matter how confident you feel, there will be times when you will need help, time, or even money from others. You will also need their friendship and support. Remember that no man is an island, and try to reciprocate any favors you are granted.

Be fanatical about the standards you intend to achieve. Never settle for "good enough" or even average attainments. Choose to be better. There is no reason you should not continually improve in every aspect of your life—and enjoy doing it. Athletes always seek to surpass their last results, to beat the present champion, and set their own world record. Actors are judged on their last performance. Authors are only as good as their last book. Adopt this same approach in every area of your life and you cannot go wrong.

Money and Your Career

It is fortunate that you are a worker because you may need to take an extra job from time to time. This is partly because you are so generous to your loved ones, but also because you can overspend on clothes and accessories when the mood hits you.

Times of Change

There are times in your life when certain planets return to the position in the sky that they occupied when you were born. It is at the times of these returns that you will consider the need for change. The two returns that will influence success in your life are the Saturn return when you are about 30 years of age and the Uranus half-return when you are about 40.

Age 25–35

For Gemini, the Saturn return usually means that you will start to look at life from a different perspective. Indeed, you will probably realize that, having sown your wild oats, you are ready to settle down to a more stable and conventional life-style. Gemini guys should perhaps begin to pay a little more attention to their partners, while Gemini ladies could well feel inspired to take up charity work or a new hobby.

Age 36–39

The Uranus half-return probably finds you feeling more mature and this will be reflected in the success you are experiencing, in both your business and private life. In fact, it could well be that even greater success is still to come. If you have not made a fortune by now, do not think it is too late. Expect the unexpected—but make sure you get your priorities right.

Age 57-60

Even though you have reached the age when many people retire, unless you are extremely well off, the chances are that you will just keep on working. This is partly because you like the independence of having enough money to spend, but also because you would soon get bored if you were not out and about among people.

Career Possibilities

1. Salesperson
2. Marketing person
3. Journalist
4. Writer
5. Magazine designer
6. Teacher
7. Babysitter
8. Sports trainer
9. Telephone operator
10. Secretary
11. Accountant
12. Banker
13. Taxi driver

14. Chauffeur
15. Racing driver
16. Civil engineer
17. Travel agent
18. Speech therapist

▶ Do What You Love Doing

The pursuit of happiness is a basic human trait. For those born under the sign of Gemini, a few special factors apply and should be remembered when you decide on your road to success. Obviously, you should do what you like doing, and wherever possible you should avoid doing what you dislike.

You like talking; indeed, you are one of nature's chatterboxes, so you need an occupation in which you have contact with other people. You dislike being confined and unable to move around freely. Yet you need a certain amount of solitude to enable you to concentrate on your work and to prevent you from wasting your time in ceaseless gossip. Novelty, variety, and change always appeal to you and you hate being kept waiting for decisions. What's more, when a decision has been reached, you like to act on it immediately, if not sooner. The best way to avoid this sort of frustration is to ensure that you are the one who makes the decisions.

One of the reasons that you tend to move around so much is that you hate being bored. Although few people want a highly pressurized job, you will do best in a career where you can be fully occupied all the time. You do not have to be tied to a desk—you would hate that. Instead, choose a career where you can work on your own initiative and at your own pace.

Gemini Health

We are all subject to colds and sneezes, but those born under the sign of Gemini tend to have more chest and throat problems than most. It annoys you when others blame your sore throats on talking too much. Remember what your mother told you when you were young and wrap up well when you go out.

Another weakness may be found in your shoulders. Beware of tasks that involve long or hard use of your shoulder muscles. Frozen shoulder is a painful ailment more associated with Gemini than any other sign due to long spells at the keyboard.

Beware of tension in your neck and shoulders. This may be nervous in origin and caused by stress. Try to remain calm and relaxed. Learn to meditate. It will help to ease all those tense muscles.

Don't let health problems go unheeded. You do tend to hide them, sometimes for too long. Then, when you do succumb, you make a terrible patient. Remember that a successful person has to be fit and healthy.

Gemini Relationships

Naturally gregarious and flirtatious, you will have a wide circle of friends. However, which of these will make your best long-term partner, in private life or in business?

Your ideal partner for love and companionship is someone born under Sagittarius—the opposite sign of the zodiac. Be honest with your partner right from the start, particularly about your past relationships. Admit, too, that you would find it intolerable if your partner tried to dominate you. More than most, you need your space. Your partner should be playful, willing to accept your practical jokes and to reciprocate in kind. Demonstrative affection is essential for Gemini, with lots of teasing, flirting, and kissing. Above all, your partner must qualify for that popular acronym "GSOH"—Good Sense of Humor. Without it your partnership is doomed.

If you are looking for passion, go for a Leo. But be warned, this may be a brief liaison before you both burn yourselves out.

You will not do better for a business partner than someone born under the sign of Libra. Here you will find a long-lasting partnership founded on a sensible footing. Libra provides the balance and stability that you need.

Gemini Positive and Negative Traits

Take your first step toward success right now. Check out the following list of Gemini positive and negative traits. Mark those that apply to you. Now start accentuating the positive and eliminating the negative.

Positive traits	Negative traits
Amusing	Aloof
Charming	Cunning
Communicative	Devious
Dexterous	Evasive
Eloquent	Fickle
Flexible	Hurtful
Friendly	Impatient
Intellectual	Impractical
Inquisitive	Indecisive
Liberal	Manipulative
Lively	Misleading
Perceptive	Sarcastic
Resourceful	Shifty
Versatile	Superficial

Over to You

You have a reputation for getting things done. That's reassuring when you are starting out on a new project. It's also a fact that you are the sort of person who will try anything once. So what's to stop you from being a success? The answer is that only you can hold yourself back. This may be a painful admission but it is a true one. You are well aware that you can quickly be bored and become impatient for results. Before you rush into any new undertaking, realize that results cannot be guaranteed and may take a long time to become apparent. Remember, too, that the new adventure on which you are starting is going to affect the rest of your life and the lives of several other people. Prepare for a long haul, take things steadily, and success is within your grasp.

4

CANCER

Main Characteristics

(Typically June 22 to July 22)

Cancer, the crab, is a cardinal water sign, a combination that produces a quite distinctive character. As is the case with all water signs, your behavior is much affected by the moon. You cling to your home like a crab to its shell. Being a cardinal sign, you demand total control of every aspect of your life, and this tends to give you tunnel vision. Once you have made a decision and have set your course, you are unlikely to be diverted. Although you appear to be in control of every situation, secretly you are highly sensitive and easily hurt. This is probably a legacy from your childhood, when you were painfully shy. You may keep your problems to yourself for too long and then take your temper and anguish out on those who are around you. Alternatively, you may be happy to talk to anyone and everyone about the things that are bothering you, and this is obviously a better line of approach. You dislike confrontation but you are not afraid of it, and you can be quite crabby if you feel even the slightest threat to your position.

You have a good memory, but may find it difficult to grasp a new concept. Like the crab, you approach things carefully, sideways, never taking things head-on. This is often linked with a profound difficulty in being impartial. Being highly emotional, the decisions you make are usually subjective. If you are sincerely seeking success, you need to deal with your feelings of insecurity and pessimism. Unless these negative traits can be controlled, they will haunt your every move and hold you back.

Cancer subjects can be slim in youth but tend to become chubby later in life, with the surplus weight settling on the top half of the body. Once people have seen your face, they rarely forget you. You probably have a larger than average head with high cheekbones and prominent brow. However, it is your expressiveness that is the most notable aspect of your appearance. Every fleeting emotion is writ large and clear on those features for anyone to read. Your clothes are likely to be simple, expensive, and in good taste and you may have a passion for all shades of blue.

THE CANCER PLAN FOR SUCCESS

Where are you now?

You will need to do a good deal of introspection to decide exactly where you are now and what you need to do before you actually start on the road to success. You do not procrastinate, but you consider that calm consideration is essential. Try to come to terms with the fact that you have to get out of your shell, leaving behind situations and possibly even several people that belong in the past who will hinder your progress. Change is inevitable when you start on the road to success, so be prepared!

New Beginnings

You may be reading this book because you have reached a stalemate in your current career or relationship. You have probably been ambitious since childhood. This urge for success, coupled with your tenacity, gives you a wonderful start. Possibly you already know which direction you would like to take but have been too timid to do anything about it. Now is the time to remember those early dreams and build on them.

One of your greatest strengths is your rich imagination, which can be a powerful tool in your search for success. If you do not recognize this as one of your qualities, think again. Perhaps your imaginative powers have been stifled or maybe they are not yet fully developed. If so, you need to develop that latent creativity. Start by taking up writing, painting, and drawing, or any other creative pastime. Read poetry, fairy stories, and sci-fi. All this will help to develop your imaginative powers, so please persevere.

You are inevitably going to need help from other people, no matter where your road to success leads. If this is the case, it will be essential that you learn to control your moods. You probably have a reputation for being ultrasensitive, touchy, and downright irritable. Have you ever stopped to consider that such behavior may frighten away people you would like to have as friends? Your intense shyness can also be a barrier to establishing relationships. Try to overcome this. If you admit to your acquaintances that shyness is a problem for you, they will understand. Other people are usually only too willing to help—but they can do so only if you let them.

Your Principles for Success

Born under the sign of Cancer, you will have no problems with your relationships within your family or your close friends. It's in that big, unknown, intimidating outside world that your problems lie.

One reason for your current lack of fulfillment is that you are haunted by a nameless fear. It's a secret that you never mention, but it's very real. No matter how great your desire for success, you are terrified of finding yourself vulnerable and unprotected in a hostile world. Even as you read those words, your heartbeat is probably quickening. The only way to deal with this is to face up to your fear! Mentally conjure up a picture of your particular gremlin, address it face-to-face and instruct it to 'Get lost!' Learn to laugh at it. Then take just one step into that supposedly hostile world, and another, and another. Fear will swiftly become a thing of the past.

Although you are good with money, you fear financial failure, especially if you are thinking in terms of a career change. The solution is simple. Sit down with pencil, paper, and your bank statements and work out your finances. Then you will be able to see whether or not you are building on a sound basis. Do this minimal amount of bookkeeping regularly, even if it's only to reassure yourself.

Now that you have learned to cope with your hidden fears, it's time to trust your sixth sense. Rely on your intuition. If a project feels right, go for it. Whatever springs to mind could turn out to be a possibility. Try following your hunches and you will probably be in for a pleasant surprise.

Don't be afraid to take risks, even though this is something you are not used to doing. If you are still scared, take some small chances first, until you get used to the idea. Risk rejection. Telephone and ask for the date you have been dreaming of. Apply for that senior post you saw advertised. What have you to lose? You could be successful—and what a boost that would be! Moreover, if it is not your lucky day, you will be no worse off than you are at present. The Universe may be waiting to give you a really big surprise, but you have to be willing to go for it.

▶ *Set Goals*

Your first step toward your new beginning is to make a list of exactly what you want out of life. Clearly spell out every objective, no matter how small or how impossible it may seem, but remember this list is not written in stone. Add to it whenever you think of something else that you would like to achieve. It's probably not a good idea to discuss your dreams with people who could dishearten you.

Why not invest in a loose-leaf file? They are inexpensive and come in a wide variety of bright colors. Then you can write each goal on a separate page, add new sheets when you have more ideas, and best of all, remove the pages as you accomplish each aim. Watch that file grow and then slim it down as you become more successful.

Finally, there is a note of warning. Be sure that the goals you set are your own. It is far too easy, especially for the young, to be influenced in this respect. Other people may be full of bright ideas and good advice—but remember that you are planning your life, not theirs. Keep your plans to yourself until you are well on the way to realizing your dreams.

▶ Where to Start

Now that you know where you are and where you want to be, it is time to start on your journey. Keep in mind that you have to play to your strengths and try to eliminate as many of your weaknesses as possible. Check out the list at the end of this chapter and be honest with yourself.

Believe in yourself and know that you can achieve what you want in life. Ensure that your goal is something you really want, not a passing fancy. Listen to your intuition and know that your success is already there—locked away in your mind. Your one primary goal incorporates your entire life, so remember to consider the improvements necessary in every department.

▶ Your Plan of Action

Mix with people who have similar interests and ambitions to your own. You can learn a lot from them. Others may try to distract you from your chosen path, but you must refuse to be influenced. Listen to what they say, then let them lead their lives the way that they want. Don't allow their problems to distract you. Avoid negative people wherever possible because they are particularly dangerous to impressionable Cancer.

You are probably not much given to thinking about the Universe. Why not start now? There is more than enough abundance in every way for everybody but you must dare to put out your hand to accept the gift. Your prosperity, happiness, health, and success will not be to the detriment of other people. Be honest in your endeavors and you will add to this Universal abundance. Perhaps that is what your ultimate aspiration should be.

Look to the future and plan for it. Release and forget past mistakes and regrets. Above all, do not feel sorry for yourself if you have experienced failure in the past. You may well have made other plans for success that came to nothing. Learn from these experiences and resolve that this time you will reach your target. The past cannot be changed, but you are opening a new door, stepping out into the future. Reinvent yourself, if necessary. Become a confident, dynamic person who gets things done.

▶ Getting It All in Focus

It is important to maintain your confidence. When you hit a problem, trust that things will work out for the best—they usually do. If a situation cannot be altered, do not worry about it. Focus on the things that can be changed to your advantage. There will be days when everything goes wrong: it happens to everybody. Don't fret about it. Go steadily about your daily work and remember that tomorrow is another day, as yet untouched. If you feel deeply depressed, ask yourself if any mistakes made today will matter tomorrow, or next week, or in a hundred years time. The answer is usually that they will not, so why worry about them?

Use your positive attributes constructively. You are an immensely caring person. Don't try to bury that sensitivity under a hard businesslike shell. You will not find success if you head off up that road. Nevertheless, guard against taking on the grief and problems of other people. Use your sensitivity in a way that is beneficial to you, as well as to others. Cancer is apt to empathize too much with other people's problems. Help where you can, but remember that other people must learn to stand on their own feet—as you have done.

It is important that you should begin each day in an upbeat mood. Start by standing in front of a mirror to reaffirm your confidence in yourself. Speaking aloud, look yourself straight in the eye and tell your reflection that today you are going to be positive in everything you say and do. Stay put until you feel confident enough to look the world in the eye in the same way. The first two or three times you do this, you may feel utterly ridiculous. Stick with it—and you will swiftly find that this routine produces results.

Periods of relaxation are vital to Cancerian well-being. Ensure that your way of life allows this.

Money and Your Career

You are inclined to be cautious where money is concerned, so you will try to manage on whatever you have, but your generosity to your family means that you sometimes find yourself a little short. In addition, when an opportunity for travel arises, you can sometimes lose all sense of proportion. For both these reasons, a job that offers a basic salary and occasional bonuses would be ideal.

Times of Change

There are times in your life when certain planets return to the position in the sky that they occupied when you were born. It is at the times of these returns that you will consider the need for changes. The two returns that will influence success in your life are the first Saturn return when you are about 30 years of age, and the Uranus half-return when you are about 40.

Age 25–35

This Saturn return seems to make many Cancer people restless and dissatisfied with what they have so far achieved. If you suddenly develop the urge to start again on a new path, give some careful thought to what you really want to do. It would be a mistake to rush into drastic changes, but this could be a turning point for you, and you need to consider the way in which you want to shape your future.

Age 36–39

In general, this Uranus half-return indicates that you should be satisfied with the way your life is turning out. So why are you feeling depressed? Right now it is important for you to take a positive view. Enjoy your happy family life, but avoid the crablike tendency to cling. Keep an open mind so far as business is concerned and try to welcome any changes that may occur.

Age 57–60

In time, your restlessness will irritate everyone around you. Look around for some paid or unpaid work that will enable you to get out and about and meet people.

Career Possibilities

1. School principal
2. Nursery teacher
3. Babysitter
4. Caregiver for the elderly
5. Caterer
6. Food manufacturer
7. Garden designer
8. Shopkeeper
9. Veterinary surgeon

10. Kennel keeper
11. Interior decorator
12. Real estate salesperson
13. Salesperson
14. Cleaner
15. Accountant
16. Sailor
17. Lifeguard
18. Insurance assessor

▶ Do What You Love Doing

You are tenderhearted and caring, so you would be well advised to choose a career in which you can use these qualities to best advantage. The only snag here is that you are so sensitive and empathic, you are likely to take on all the problems and traumas you encounter in your line of duty. You could be highly successful in any caring profession, but be warned of the toll it may take on your own health and emotions.

If, as previously advised, you have cultivated your rich imagination, you could look for success as a writer or publicist. Add your love of gourmet foods to your cooking skills and you may find an outlet for your talents.

You could become a successful art teacher and would probably revel in the work. There is no better way to learn a subject than to teach it. Your own artistic ability could blossom under these circumstances.

Check out your talents again and combine them with those things you would really love to do. It is by combining these sometimes disparate elements that you will find success.

Cancer Health

Digestive problems may be your Achilles heel. It's a pity that you love your food so much, because this tendency can lead to a number of problems. What happens if you experience a stomach upset? You worry about it, and worry and stress are the prime causes of stomach ulcers.

If you want to stay healthy, avoid eating disorders. These include overeating or starving yourself so that you become undernourished. It also means being careful about what you eat—we are talking quality here, as well as quantity. Simple, fresh food in reasonable quantities suits your metabolism. Your taste for rich foods can lead to weight problems.

Try to maintain a steady eating pattern, regulating your calorie intake. You are liable to indulge in "comfort eating," running to the refrigerator for another cream cake whenever somebody or something upsets you. Comfort eating equals more food that equals more weight, more stress, and more stomach problems. The cycle then continues into more worry and more comfort eating.

Cancer Relationships

Cancer needs a partner, perhaps more than any other sign in the zodiac. Without one, success will be difficult to achieve. You are an extremely faithful person and, once a partnership has been formed, it is likely to continue indefinitely.

An ideal partner in your personal life is somebody born under the sign of Taurus. You will be well matched in your love of home life and share the same ideas on how that home should look. Your intuitive understanding of each other will help you over any difficulties that may arise. Spending time together will be important to both of you. When the children arrive, they will be welcomed and loved. This, indeed, could be a marriage made in heaven.

In your business life you will do no better than to find someone born under the sign of Scorpio. You will have so many complementary attributes that this partnership is bound to be harmonious and fruitful. Scorpio subjects will understand your moods, will accept the criticism that you find difficult, and—unlike you—will remain calm in a crisis.

Cancer Positive and Negative Traits

Take your first step toward success right now. Check out the following list of Cancer positive and negative traits. Mark those that apply to you. Now start accentuating the positive and eliminating the negative.

Positive traits	Negative traits
Adaptable	Antisocial
Caring	Argumentative
Cautious	Changeable
Compassionate	Defensive
Dependable	Dependent
Domesticated	Devious
Faithful	Hoarding
Imaginative	Manipulative
Intuitive	Moody
Kind	Oversensitive
Protective	Pessimistic
Sensitive	Prejudiced
Shrewd	Selfish
Tenacious	Touchy

Over to You

Those born under the sign of Cancer are usually deep thinkers and you are much given to analysis. This means that you will not be deterred by the amount of introspection required before you can reach a decision about your future.

You need to reevaluate your lifestyle and yourself. Try to become more objective in your outlook and learn to let go of the past. Grit your teeth and accept constructive criticism gracefully. Realize that if you are to achieve the success you want, you must come out from under your protective shell and be part of twenty-first century living. You can do it.

5

LEO

Main Characteristics

(Typically July 23 to August 22)

Leo is the fixed fire sign of the zodiac, producing a rare combination of traits that make you the strong character that you are. Natives of this sign are also exceptionally ambitious. For you, success is the grail you seek.

Fixed and fire may seem like conflicting terms, because those with fixed qualities are seen as stable and cautious while fire people are expected to be enthusiastic and energetic. However, Leo's blaze is controlled, like a homely log fire. Its light helps to keep you out of the shadows, which is a good thing for you as you are no shrinking violet. You love the limelight; in fact, most Leos are born extroverts. You want to be center stage all the time, or you're not playing. Your vitality, enthusiasm, and a marked practical streak combine to produce your powerful, dynamic personality. You are the Lion, the king of your own particular jungle. You are so independent that you are not much of a team worker. You even prefer sporting activities that are more like single combat than being part of a team.

You probably hold a high opinion of yourself, but you should try to hide this. Your obvious self-esteem can make others see you as arrogant, self-satisfied, and stubborn. They would be surprised to learn that you actually need large servings of reassurance and praise. An adoring audience is vital to you, and it nurtures your confidence. When you feel on top of things, your sunny disposition, honesty, and loyalty come to the fore.

True to your fiery qualities, you like to get on and change things—not tomorrow or the next day, but NOW. This trait will be useful to you in your search for success, but try to keep it under control. Your inborn Leo energy can be somewhat alarming to less forceful people. You are a natural organizer and also a good teacher. You plan and prepare properly for the classes or teaching that you give.

You recognize the importance of first impressions. So your clothing is stylish, expensive, and often a little flamboyant. Determined to be noticed, you wear bright colors—yellows, gold, and red or perhaps nothing but dramatic black. Ever the showman, your appearance is usually immaculate and you are not averse to spending a lot of money on your appearance.

THE LEO PLAN FOR SUCCESS

Where are you now?

Why are you reading this book? Perhaps it is because you currently lack the appreciation that you regard as your birthright. For you, status is more important than cash in the bank. Constant attention is essential. You simply cannot function without it. In every aspect of your life, you demand being allowed to use your qualities and to be applauded for them. If your current situation does not allow scope for your enthusiasm and talent, it must be changed. Make no mistake; this is important.

New Beginnings

Making a fresh start is challenging; consider your strengths and how you can build on them. What about your weaknesses? Even lion kings have faults that they can work on. Despite your hidden insecurity, you are reluctant to admit to weaknesses, but if you are aiming for success, you must be prepared to confess your limitations—if only to yourself.

If you are sincerely seeking success, you need to examine your likes and dislikes. Success in your private life and in your career is more probable if you are happy with what you are doing. You do best when doing something you enjoy. A partner who enjoys quiet evenings watching romantic videos is not for you. Neither will you enjoy a plodding desk-bound job. Leo wants to be on the move, mentally and physically.

Though you need an admiring group of friends, you must also pay attention to your critics. As a true Leo, you may be so blinded by your own light that you cannot see the shadows. Allow others to point them out to you. Don't be so sensitive about your image that you are afraid of losing face. Your critics may also be friends and fans who are trying to help you. Self-esteem is one thing, but vanity and conceit are something else.

If you are seeking financial success, then you will need to examine your spending habits. You are generous to a fault and love to spend what you have, making a show and being extravagant. Try to curb this tendency so that you are not constantly struggling to stay out of debt. If you are already in the red, do something about it, so that you can start your new life on a firm footing.

On the positive side, you are a great organizer and you can plan a campaign or an event so that it works.

Your Principles for Success

Be aware that your fiery nature and your urge for instant action may militate against you. You see opportunities, you grab them, and you make the most of them. Very few people can do this. They do not have your courage, and going after success is not necessarily part of their karma. Remember this if you become frustrated by the lack of ability or ambition that others seem to display. Some Leos lack patience, so if you are in the habit of getting started on something before reading the instructions, slow down and think a little first.

Not everyone is as creative, extrovert, and quick to act as you are. You see opportunities and go after them, and while others are happy to allow them to pass, many people will be happy to follow your path. You enjoy showing others how things should be done and are generous with your praise and compliments. Try not to be scornful and intolerant of those who are slower than you. Respect those who are better informed than you are and do not try to cut them down to size. Use all the help you can get when you are on the way up. You may need those friends again later if you take a tumble.

Remember that respect must be earned and that leadership also has its obligations. One of the best ways to earn the respect of others is to take time to listen to them. Try to curb your indifference or impatience. Listen with your heart as well as your mind.

▶ Set Goals

The first step on your road to success is to identify your goals. Decide what success means to you and exactly what you want in life. Then analyze your goals—are they feasible? If so, what time scale will be necessary to reach them? Is it is possible to work toward several goals simultaneously or will each have to take its turn? If so, how will you prioritize them? Take the long-term view, decide on your ultimate aim, then work back from there. What intermediate goals will you need to achieve on the way? Then decide what you need to do before you can attain those midway goals. These are the minor but essential goals you can work toward immediately.

Writing down your goals has several advantages:

- You will be clear about the direction you are taking.

- You will have a sense of purpose in what you are doing.

- You will make the best use of your time—with no dead-end diversions.

- The list will help to maintain your enthusiasm.

- It will boost your confidence.

- You will be able to monitor your progress.

- You will be in total control—something of primary importance to Leo.

▶ *Where to Start*

It is vital that you should recognize your true worth because, despite your apparent confidence, this does not come easily to you. Your confident attitude is often a disguise for your innate insecurity. Harboring doubts but denying them, even to yourself, will handicap you in your quest. Confide your new ideas to someone you can trust. Seek their advice, particularly concerning your misgivings about your own abilities. Ask them to support you and occasionally, when necessary, give you a push. This kind of support and encouragement is essential to Leo, and it is here that a loving partner is a crucial component of your success.

You will never achieve anything until you realize that you must settle to a steady rate of progress. Don't rush at everything, because that could be a disaster. Even though you are a born leader, you are still learning. Be content with being top of the class, not the tutor.

It's no bad thing to be conservative, especially in business. Being the extrovert showman may go down well in your private life. In other areas, it can be unacceptable. Learn to curb your extremist ideas. New bosses do not take kindly to militant employees making revolutionary suggestions.

▶ Your Plan of Action

What is the reason for your doubts about your own abilities? Could it be that you realize that you lack knowledge? Perhaps you need certain qualifications. If this is the case, you should immediately set about obtaining them. This must be your first priority in your plan of action. No matter how able you are, paper qualifications are essential in the business world. They should not be difficult to get. There are so many diverse methods of learning whatever skills are needed that anyone of any age can gain any credentials required. Leos often do quite badly at school. This is due to the fact that they can be up to twelve months younger than the other pupils in their year. Many need an extra year at college, while others take up some form of education later in life when they know what it is that they need to study.

In the beginning, you are going to need a team. Of course, you will want to be the leader, but if another member is better qualified than you, have the grace to yield to him—at least initially. The time will come when, having learned all you need, you can take over. Ensure that your team members are completely reliable. Loyalty is one of your strengths. Don't allow it to be undermined by the disloyalty of others. At all costs, guard against the formation of cliques or any kind of underhanded activity.

▶ Getting It All in Focus

Life's journey is full of ups and downs—for all of us. Most people understand this but you, as a Leo, are unable to even consider the idea of failure. Ridicule would be even harder for you to bear. It is important to understand that in your quest for success there will be times when you will fail. You like a gamble, so take one with your success strategy. It's no different than placing a bet on a horse—you only do it when you know you can afford to lose. A failure is only a loss of time— and tomorrow is another day when you can try again.

In planning your route to success, it is important to analyze each new factor that you come across. Is it crucial to your plan of action? Avoid indecision. There are no gray areas here. You have to decide whether to take action immediately or to discard the idea and avoid wasting time.

Making a new start will probably require you to take orders from someone else. You will also need to accept some constructive criticism, which does not come easily to Leo. Try to remember that it is an essential step toward getting everything in focus.

Money and Your Career

There is no doubt about it; you can spend money in style, so there is no point in your looking for anything but a well paid top job! This is not only because you are happiest when flying by the seat of your pants, but also because your need for luxury and glamour demands a high income.

Times of Change

There are times in your life when certain planets return to the position in the sky that they occupied when you were born. It is at the times of these returns that you will consider the need for change. The two returns that will influence success in your life are the first Saturn return when you are about 30 years of age, and the Uranus half-return when you are about 40.

Age 25–35

At the time of the Saturn return, you begin to take a good look at yourself and your world, and you may not be too pleased with what you see. You hate to admit defeat, but it may be time to acknowledge that a partnership—be it business or emotional—just is not working out. You will need to make some far-reaching decisions; then things will work out with surprising ease.

Age 36–39

This is the time when Leo can experience a certain loss of confidence in several areas. The Uranus half-return could make you worry about your work, your partnerships, and even your appearance. Think carefully and objectively about all this. If changes need to be made, your courage and self-confidence will enable you to make the right decisions and to carry them through.

Age 57–60

Puttering around at home is not for you, so you will either continue to work at your usual job or look around for something else. If you absolutely have to give up working, you will become involved in your local amateur dramatic society or something else of the kind.

Career Possibilities

1. Office manager
2. Business manager
3. Company director
4. Factory manager
5. Event organizer
6. Actor
7. Dancer
8. Entertainer
9. Interior designer
10. Dress designer
11. Salesperson
12. Jewelry dealer
13. Computer whiz
14. Nursery teacher
15. Writer
16. Legal secretary
17. Trades union negotiator
18. Astrologer

▶ Do What You Love Doing

You need appreciation, and you love working with other people, so how about a classroom full of children to keep in order? Any teaching position would suit you. However, you must go further than this. What are you going to teach? Teach what you love doing.

Top of your list of congenial occupations are theater and drama. It could well be that you dream of becoming a director or producer in the theater, films, or television. Equally, the captive audience to be found in a court of law may attract you. Imagine yourself as an attorney, with judge and jury hanging on your every word.

The Leo love of sport could lead to a satisfying career as a coach. Salesmanship is another possibility for you, using your ability to communicate, display your expertise to a captive audience, and charm prospective customers.

Oddly enough, while you are probably interested in the hands-on side of engineering, you feel comfortable with computers, so computer-aided engineering and design could be a good career.

No matter which career you decide upon, be sure that it fulfills the following criteria:

- ▶ Your friendly, outgoing personality is appreciated.

- ▶ Some form of emotional involvement is required.

- ▶ You are respected for your powers of leadership.

- ▶ You can demonstrate and make use of your creative talents.

- ▶ You are able to help others in some way.

- ▶ You get the praise you deserve when you do the job well.

- ▶ Success is assured if you are happy in your career.

Leo Health

You are likely to lead a stressful life, bearing in mind your need for love and appreciation and your constant struggle for supremacy.

Stress may lead to heart trouble—always a danger for those born under the sign of Leo. Strive to keep calm. Monitor your blood pressure, and watch your diet. In situations that start your heart racing, slow down, or sit down and relax until your heartbeat returns to normal. Learn to concentrate on your breathing to ease stress.

Leo tends to suffer from back problems. Poor posture, bad lifting technique, and overexertion can worsen this. Unfortunately, some back problems seem to appear without reason. Resist your natural inclination to push-start a car or carry a piano upstairs. The truth is, your spirit is more than willing, but your back is weak. Rather, you can advise on how the job can best be done.

Exercise is important for you. Cycling and swimming are particularly beneficial, enabling you to enjoy physical activity without strain. Both these sports can satisfy your competitive instincts. Running, tennis, or squash are bad choices once you are past the age of 30, as landing heavily on your feet can jar your spine.

When you are unwell, you are a terrible patient, anxious to be up and about before you are physically able. Try to control this impatience. Accept that you need to rest until you have fully recuperated. This is common sense, not weakness.

Leo Relationships

If you care to refer to the Aries section of this book, you will find that the ideal partner there is Leo. It follows that Aries is the perfect partner for you. You are a wonderful lover, making your partner feel really special. Such behavior is natural to you and cannot be classed as acting. Be sure that your partner realizes that friendship and unconditional love are as important to you as sex. You can also relate to the air signs of Gemini, Libra, and Aquarius, while many of you appreciate the sense of humor and loyalty of Scorpio.

In business, your partner needs to be in some way subordinate to you. Remember, too, your need for praise and support. Someone born under the sign of Libra is likely to have the understanding, balanced nature you require.

In both your private life and in business, select your partner with care. You, above all others, will be devastated by betrayal in any shape or form.

Leo Positive and Negative Traits

Self-assessment is difficult for you, so if necessary, ask the help of an advisor. Your friends may see you more clearly than you see yourself.

Check out the following list of positive and negative Leo traits. Mark those that apply to you. Now start accentuating the positive and eliminating the negative.

Positive traits	Negative traits
Affectionate	Arrogant
Ambitious	Boastful
Creative	Bossy
Dignified	Conceited
Dramatic	Dogmatic
Enterprising	Intolerant
Faithful	Overbearing
Generous	Patronizing
Loving	Pompous
Loyal	Pretentious
Magnanimous	Stubborn
Noble	Unrealistic
Proud	Vain
Romantic	Willful

Over to You

Always be totally honest with yourself. If all is not going well in your quest for success, try to find out why. If necessary, try asking trusted friends. This is when you have to be prepared for constructive criticism; as you are asking for it, you should be prepared to accept it. You find it difficult to accept advice or criticism but, if you are not achieving your goals, you need to bite the bullet. Find a person you can use as your sounding board and—if necessary—as your mentor. Above all, listen to what you are told and do not dismiss advice simply because it does not fit in with your own ideas. There are times, believe it or not, when other people know best.

6

VIRGO

Main Characteristics

(Typically August 13 to September 11)

Virgo is a mutable earth sign of the zodiac, and this combination of qualities produces a practical and adaptable temperament. One of your peculiarities is that you tend to deny your characteristics. Let's begin with one you cannot refute—then you will be more likely to accept what follows.

You are fastidious regarding cleanliness, hygiene, and health. In this respect, as in all others, you strive for perfection. You have an attractive personality—witty, charming, and lively. Others regard you as efficient, shrewd, and logical. Nevertheless, how do you see yourself? It's probable that you worry more than most about the areas in life where you feel that you are failing. You often feel that you are not good enough for your job or your partner.

This lack of self-esteem makes you somewhat introverted, so you seldom seek the spotlight, preferring to work conscientiously behind the scenes. This is actually a strength rather than a weakness, because painstaking types like you are just as valuable as the firebrands of this world.

A typical Virgo is consistently immaculate. You carry yourself well, projecting an aura of dignity and self-assurance. Your hair will be well groomed, showing off your large forehead. Depending upon your racial background, you probably have soft gray or blue eyes. Clothes in natural earth colors appeal to you, but you probably choose gray or black for formal events. Whatever you wear will be stylish, of excellent quality, and appropriate for the occasion.

THE VIRGO PLAN FOR SUCCESS

Where are you now?

Right now, you may be stuck in a dead-end job where you are simply taken for granted. Your perfectionist streak probably means you are the most efficient person in the company, but you seldom recognize your own worth. If you want success, you must stop being self-critical and learn to assert yourself. You also fear insecurity and for this reason, you find it difficult to cope with change. Nevertheless, you may have to change if you are to have the success you are seeking.

New Beginnings

Making changes does not mean altering your basic personality; all you need to do is to develop your positive points. In this respect you have plenty going for you. Acknowledge that you have many good attributes. At the end of this chapter you will find a list of 14 such traits—all yours. They already exist within you, but you must develop them. At the same time, face up to the negative characteristics that tend to hold you back. This will not be easy, but you are not one to shirk a task, so you will conscientiously tackle it.

To obtain success you must be prepared for change, lots of it. Don't try to do everything at once. Imagine success as an island set in a lake, so you will need lots of stepping-stones to reach it. If you think you can make it in one jump, you will probably drown. Be prepared for floods and tempests along the way. Nothing worth having is ever achieved without problems of one kind or another, and the end result will be all the more valuable owing to the difficulties you face up to and overcome.

Your Principles for Success

Virgo is a natural-born analyst. This, in addition to your urge for perfection, produces the constant self-criticism that can make your life so difficult. Your tendency to criticize can make other people's lives difficult too, so learn to control it. Focus your critical abilities on things and situations, rather than on people. Your clear thinking can be extremely helpful to others but all too often you express your thoughts in too blunt a manner. This antagonizes the very people you are trying to help—and do not forget that you may need their assistance at some time in the future. Make a real effort to overcome this tendency.

Virgo is definitely the zodiac's worrier par excellence. You worry about your health to the point that others may consider you a hypochondriac. You worry about your own perceived shortcomings. You worry about money—or the lack of it. Even when all is going well, you worry because you are sure the good times cannot last. Pause for a moment and think about this. You have been worrying all your life. Has that worrying had any effect on the outcome of any situation? Of course it hasn't—so you must stop aggravating yourself in this way.

The antidote to worry is relaxation. The mere mention of the word is likely to send Virgo into a tailspin, but you need to overcome your conviction that there is something almost sinful about it. Your current idea of relaxation is probably to take an hour off on Sunday morning instead of working all weekend. Change your views. Set aside some time at least once a week during which you can relax with family and friends. You will undoubtedly feel the benefit of this—so do not worry about it.

▶ Set Goals

When you check on your positive traits that are listed at the end of this section, you will notice the same number of negative qualities alongside them. What are you going to do about these? Don't be tempted to deny that you exhibit the negative traits. Instead, admit that most of them apply to you to at least some extent. Your immediate goal is to eradicate or learn to control them. The easiest and most effective way to do this is to use affirmations. An affirmation is an assertion that the desired state already exists. To start with, equip yourself with a set of small index cards, then decide which of the listed negative traits is causing you the most problems. Perhaps you tend to be irritable when things do not go the way you want. Take a pen and print clearly on one of the file cards "I am patient and serene at all times." Now place the card where you will see it every day. Some people make several copies—one propped against the bedside clock, one beside the bathroom mirror, one taped to the computer monitor. Repeat the affirmation, both silently and aloud, as frequently as you can. Write it down ten times whenever you find yourself with a pen in your hand.

Your Virgo cynicism will probably reject this idea, but try it anyway. You probably will not realize how effective affirmations can be until a friend remarks that you seem to be less irritable. When that happens, you can go on to deal with the next negative trait on your list. After a while, you may even find it fun. You will certainly have discovered a weapon for dealing with many of your disappointments and inadequacies. Affirmations are important—and they work.

▶ Where to Start

By now you probably know a great deal more about yourself than you did previously, so you will wonder when you are going to start on the road to success. First, you must have a specific destination in mind. If you simply set off on a journey with no clear idea of where you are going, you will land up in "Never Never Land," and that's a dream world where nothing real ever happens.

Be precise about your final destination. Do you want to be the boss of the business in which you are currently employed? Would you like to be a champion athlete? Alternatively, is it your aim to maintain a thriving personal relationship? Success comes in many guises and it does not necessarily involve money. What you can achieve is limited only by your own imagination and determination. Aim for only one goal at a time, but give your all to achieving it.

Employ your Virgo logic in considering the areas in which you would like to succeed. Assess the cons as well as the pros. If you do not possess the qualifications for the position you are seeking, set about obtaining them. If you need more money, take advice from financial experts on how best to obtain it. As the Chinese say, a journey of a thousand miles starts with a single step. However great the temptation, do not rush blindly ahead and take chances. Make a plan of action and stick with it.

▶ Your Plan of Action

As a Virgo, you have a marked tendency to shoot yourself in the foot. You are always doing it, aren't you? In fact, this is an area where you tend to be your own worst enemy. Avoid stress. It leads to tension, and that leads to nervous exhaustion. How are you going to make important business decisions if you are so tired that you cannot think straight? Don't imagine that working under constant pressure is part and parcel of success. You cannot do everything yourself, so you must learn to delegate. Then when you have really important decisions to make, you will be capable of dealing with them.

It's important, too, that you recognize certain traits, good or bad, in others, so become a people watcher. Get into the habit of assessing others and understanding what makes them tick. Control your natural critical attitude and do not take anything or anybody at face value. Determine that once you have made a decision you will stick with it because inconsistency is not conducive to good business. Keep an open mind about suggestions from other people. Your tendency to be dogmatic can alienate those who are in a position to help you.

▶ Getting It All in Focus

If you are to achieve the success that you desire, you will need a psychological makeover. Develop confidence in yourself and your abilities. Throw out all your old excuses and eliminate the word *can't* from your vocabulary. You can do virtually anything if you muster the courage to try. For you, fear can become a self-fulfilling prophecy. Your own special gremlins are fear of failure and your lack of self-esteem.

These gremlins can be dealt with simply by taking responsibility for your own convictions. Harbor thoughts of failure and you will fail, but develop a positive self-image and you will succeed. It really is as simple as that. If you find it difficult to convince yourself that you are on the road to success, go back to your affirmation cards for help. You are a lively communicator, but you must beware of telling all and sundry about your plans for the future. The danger is that your subconscious will think that you have already accomplished your task and thus allow you to let it slip. Cherish your dreams in private. Tell others only when you have achieved your objectives.

Don't be tempted to cut corners in order to finish a task quickly. Virgos tend to move swiftly from one job to the next, and sometimes you do not close one door properly before opening the next. Take your time.

Money and Your Career

You are not noted for being a big spender, so a job that brings in a steady but reasonable income is fine. You do need to watch your spending on small items though, such as books and CDs, as these can add up and catch you out from time to time.

Times of Change

There are times in your life when certain planets return to the position in the sky that they occupied when you were born. It is at the times of these returns that you will consider the need for change. The two returns that will influence success in your life are the first Saturn return when you are about 30 years of age and the Uranus half-return when you are about 40.

Age 25–35

Your first Saturn return is likely to have a somewhat disruptive effect on your life. You may be fretting against various limitations that you are experiencing. Maybe you should stop banging your head against a brick wall and look for another more satisfactory way to get to the other side of your problems. Perhaps you have reached a crossroads in your life. Think carefully, take a positive approach, and step out boldly on a new path.

Age 36–39

By the time of your Uranus half-return you should have realized that positive action is more likely to produce results than worrying. Now is the time to take definite steps to ensure that your life is running the way you want it to. If you do not, you could end up a bitter and disappointed oldster. You can avoid that fate simply by broadening your horizons and taking a fresh look at life.

Age 57–60

A Virgo who has nothing to do is a contradiction in terms, so you will either stay on at work or retire from your main job and take on something new. This may well be something that serves your local community in some way.

Career Possibilities

1. Doctor
2. Nurse
3. Hospital administrator
4. Alternative therapist
5. Herbalist
6. Forensic expert
7. Statistician
8. Computer analyst
9. Financial analyst
10. Clerk
11. Engineer
12. Secretary
13. Personnel manager
14. Taxi driver
15. Writer
16. Publisher
17. Editor
18. Astrologer

▶ Do What You Love Doing

Your quest for success may demand a change of profession. If so, be sure to choose a job that you enjoy. You dislike almost any form of change, so the new position must be one to which you can look forward with confidence.

Try to find work that will combine your positive traits with something you enjoy doing. As a simple example, your perfectionist streak and your love of nature could merge with your liking for routine into a career as a horticulturist.

You enjoy working with words, charts, and maps, so you could write successful gardening books that include illustrations and descriptions of plants and layouts. Gardening books come second only to cook books in popularity. If you do not fancy writing, but you love books, how about becoming an editor? This job requires exactly the qualities that you have, these being patience, an eye for detail, and a love of words.

Virgo is an earth sign, which may mean that you prefer the natural way of doing things and may be drawn to some form of holistic or complementary medicine. As this profession requires care, precision, and concern for others, it should suit you well.

Many Virgos are not interested in being their own boss. If this is true of you, your success may lie in an essential supporting role that will make good use of your own special attributes. Your scientific mind might take you into space technology or genetic engineering. These careers demand workers who are meticulous, analytical, and logical, and who enjoy complicated but routine work. In other words, such positions seem tailor-made for you.

Whatever new career you choose, never be tempted to take on an extra position in order to make ends meet or to see how a new career might work out before you jump ship. For a Virgo this could spell disaster. You need to focus entirely on whatever you are doing, and trying to cope with two jobs at once could make you overwrought.

Virgo Health

Your physical health is very much bound up with your mental attitude. As mentioned earlier, others may see you as a hypochondriac because you worry so much about every little ache or pain. Your obsession with hygiene and cleanliness ensures that you cannot bear the idea of being ill. For this reason, you do look after yourself more than most, which means that you avoid many common ailments. When you do fall sick you are quick to search your well-stocked medicine cabinet for an appropriate remedy.

Most Virgo health problems are caused by worry. You are likely to suffer from insomnia. You worry all night and get up the next morning feeling headachy and prickly. In consequence, you lose patience with others and your irritability takes over. Try meditation or some other relaxation technique to help you wind down at the end of the day.

Physically, you may be prone to problems of the abdomen or lower bowel. A good balanced diet is essential if you are to avoid bouts of diarrhea. Intense discomfort after eating may also be a problem. Green vegetables and fresh fruit should constitute the staple items of your diet.

Virgo Relationships

As a well-organized, considerate and industrious person, it is important that you find a partner who shares the same characteristics. This may suggest that a fellow Virgo would be ideal. The truth is that a Virgo partner could be suitable but might not exactly be the best choice. You will be too similar in too many ways, especially sharing negative traits that you want to play down.

In both your private and your professional life, your soul mate may well be a Capricorn. Here you will find someone whose positive characteristics are very similar to your own. You will feel at ease in this relationship and able to be completely open and honest with one another. In business, your Capricorn partner will work as hard as you do and enjoy the achievements that you both make. In your private life, Capricorn will supply the love, devotion, and attention that you crave, and your partner will not let you down when you are most in need of support. Immediate and strong attraction between Virgo and Capricorn is not unusual—sometimes it's called love at first sight.

Virgo Positive and Negative Traits

As you now know, Virgo may have several negative traits, but these are outweighed by your many positive qualities. However, you need to be constantly alert—particularly when things are not going well—if you are to prevent those negative characteristics from resurfacing. Remember your need for periods of relaxation. Use affirmations to deal with practically any problem that may arise. Finally, check out the following list of positive and negative Virgo traits. Mark those that apply to you. Now start accentuating the positive and eliminating the negative.

Positive traits	Negative traits
Analytical	Cynical
Considerate	Dogmatic
Discreet	Eccentric
Discriminating	Fussy
Efficient	Hypochondriac
Industrious	Inconsistent
Intelligent	Irritable
Logical	Negative
Methodical	Nervous
Modest	Obsessive
Painstaking	Overcritical
Practical	Pedantic
Scholarly	Prudish
Shy	Untidy

Over to You

Now it is up to you. Only you can implement the changes that have been outlined here. It will not be easy, but you should not doubt your ability to reach your goal. Though you now recognize your negative traits, you no longer try to justify them. Instead, you employ your positive qualities to the fullest. If you have followed the suggestions in this book, you will certainly feel more confident and less self-critical. Nowadays you tend to see every obstacle as a challenge, something to overcome and to learn from. Never look back. The new bright, glorious future to which you aspire is there, waiting for you. Go forward with confidence and claim your reward.

7

LIBRA

Main Characteristics

(Typically September 23 to October 22)

Libra is the cardinal air sign of the zodiac, so it produces an individual who is highly efficient at putting ideas into action. Air people are dynamic, but they do not always seize the opportunity while the going is good. You understand the latest technology and delight in using it to best advantage. As a cardinal sign, you are also enterprising and ambitious. Libra has great potential for bringing about and using the changes that can lead to success.

Your zodiac symbol is the scales, so this denotes that you seek balance in all situations. You tend to sit on the fence, weighing up all the pros and cons before making a decision. This has advantages and disadvantages. You see both sides of any argument and this tendency, together with your reluctance to commit yourself, can infuriate some people. However, once you have reached a decision, that's it! No amount of persuasion will make you change your mind. Decisions made by Librans are set in stone, despite your apparently changeable tendencies.

You hate discord and conflict of any kind and do not take kindly to those who cause it. This means that you sometimes harbor grudges for an unnecessarily long time. On the other hand you can be diplomatic, reasonable, and impartial. You like a peaceful life and you are usually soft-spoken, which is a factor that can lend authority to anything you say.

In many ways, your appearance reflects your sign, being well balanced and almost symmetrical. You are usually cheerful, and when you smile the whole room lights up. Dimples in your chin or cheeks may emphasize this smile.

When choosing clothes you always strive for balance and harmony. You would never wear anything that could be described as being in poor taste. Subtle shades suit you best and you like all tones of blue, from the palest aqua to the darkest navy.

THE LIBRA PLAN FOR SUCCESS

Where are you now?

Are you sitting on the fence, in typical Libra fashion, unsure which way to jump? Are you waiting for someone else to make the first move? There's nothing wrong with this attitude, but there are times when you need a metaphorical wake-up call and a good shaking before you will get off that fence to make those changes.

New Beginnings

Once you have decided on an aim in life, you will need to take positive action—and that is almost certain to unsettle the balance of your Libra scales. Don't be alarmed. When you discard something from one side of the scales, the balance can be restored by replacing it with another item. In other words, you will have to make changes that may temporarily throw you off balance, but equilibrium will swiftly be restored.

First among these changes will be your habits of thought. Certain characteristics are natural to anyone born under the sign of Libra, but you may not be aware of them until they are pointed out. Others who know you well are likely to be more knowledgeable about your idiosyncrasies.

Now is the time for you to recognize these inborn traits, to discard or moderate the ones that will hinder your progress and to cultivate those that will help you.

Like us all, you do have some weaknesses, but you also have some useful attributes. You are an excellent communicator and mediator. When you want to, you can charm the birds from the trees, but you must take care how you use that charisma. Don't be tempted to use it to manipulate other people. Eventually they will realize what you are doing and they will never trust you again. It is important that you should acknowledge and deal with your negative traits. If you do not, they will hold you back from attaining the goal you seek.

Your Principles for Success

Have you heard of creative visualization? It's a mind game that will help you a great deal in your quest for success. You can practice it at any time under almost any circumstances. All you have to do is create a mental picture of what life will be like when you have achieved your objective. Close your eyes and see yourself as the person you would like to be, enjoying the fruits of your success. Visualize your new home in detail. See yourself confidently carrying out your business obligations. Build up a vivid image of your perfect partner and the sort of social life you will enjoy. Before you open your eyes, pause a moment longer and affirm, "Yes! This is how it's going to be." Believe, and it will happen. You are, in fact, creating your own reality.

Visualization will produce aims you had not even thought about. Some people keep a scrapbook in which they paste pictures of everything they want. Try it—and look at it frequently. Anything that keeps your ambitions and their attainment in the forefront of your mind is important. Become fixated on your success to the exclusion of all else.

▶ Set Goals

Unless you aim for some definite targets on the road to success, you will never achieve anything. First, you must decide exactly what you want. What does success mean to you? Is it a bigger house, more time to spend with your family, a new car, sorting out your den, or simply peace and quiet away from the rat race? Make a list. Set down anything and everything that you equate with success. Don't rush it. Keep adding to the list as more ideas come to mind. Then, when you really cannot think of anything more, rewrite the list in order of priority. You will find that positive action—even something as slight as writing down a list—reinforces your determination.

Next, make a realistic deadline for the achievement of each goal. It's no good wanting everything yesterday, or even this afternoon. Think carefully about how long it will take you to achieve each step on the road to success. Obviously, it will not take five years to sort out your den, but neither will you gain essential qualifications overnight. Don't be so carried away with enthusiasm that you demand too much of yourself. You will end up disappointed and disheartened.

▶ Where to Start

Having decided on your precise objectives, you must consider how you are going to achieve them. Make this a firm commitment. Don't shout it from the rooftops, though. Confide in the important people in your life, explaining what you are doing and why you are doing it. Hopefully they will lend you their support. You will need all the help you can get in terms of understanding and time—and maybe some financial support, too.

This full-time dedication means that you will be pretty hyped up as you start on your quest. That's fine, but don't overdo it. Take one step at a time. Complete the current task before you embark on another. Take time out to relax and recharge your batteries. When you have achieved a goal, however minor, acknowledge it with a small celebration—perhaps a family meal or a day out.

Be persistent. Once you have started making changes in your life, stick with them and maintain your enthusiasm. If you realize you are sinking back into your old habits, spend more time in visualization. Reread this section and reinvigorate your enthusiasm.

You want to get lucky? The harder you work, the luckier you will become. Sometimes, when the going gets tough, you will want to opt out. Don't even think about it. You are the only person who can succeed in this venture and you are also the only one who can fail, so it's up to you, isn't it?

Add one more skill to those you already possess. Learn to be responsive. Listen, observe, and be aware of what others are saying and doing. Librans sometimes prefer to talk rather than to listen, and even worse, some talk at people rather than *to* them. Ask questions. Most people enjoy giving advice. Learn from others. Then build on what you have learned and move forward.

▶ Your Plan of Action

At the end of each day, take time to assess your accomplishments, your mistakes, and the lessons that you have learned. This daily self-analysis is vital to your progress. Without it, you will drift back into your old habit of assuming that all's well with your world.

Start on a positive note and write down what you have accomplished. No matter how minor that success may seem, make a note of it. Give yourself some small reward, a chocolate or a beer, according to your taste. But don't cheat! If you have not made any progress in your quest for success, abstain.

What have you learned? Write down the details. New facts are all too easily buried beneath the wealth of knowledge you already possess. Why not enter newly acquired information in an indexed notebook, so that you can easily access it when needed?

What mistakes have you made? Be aware that you will fail at times because we all do. Accept your failures philosophically but be sure to learn from them. When a setback occurs, ask yourself why. Determine what you can do to turn that failure into a success. If that is not possible, resolve to avoid that pitfall in the future. Above all, never permit an error of judgment to deter you from pressing on—and never attempt to blame other people for your mistakes.

▶ Getting It All in Focus

Emphasize your positive qualities. Use them to your advantage. You are probably the sort of person who detests noisy arguments, but it's almost inevitable that you will be faced with aggression at some time in your career. This is the time to use that charm of yours. Listen while your antagonist blows his top, and then quietly and calmly make your point. You will win, hands down, every time. What's more, you will gain the respect of more hotheaded types.

It is possible to change your negative traits into positive ones. You may lack confidence in yourself and your poor self image can be reinforced when things go wrong. Ignore the inner voice that tells you that you are not as nice, as clever, or as well liked as you wish to be. The bottom line is that if you do not love yourself, you can never truly love anyone else. This is where visualization proves useful. At least once a day, create a mental image of yourself as confident, popular, and efficient. Try doing this last thing at night, just as you are dropping off to sleep. The next morning, you will feel better and you will be ready to tackle anything fate sends you. If you persist in these small exercises, you will be surprised at how quickly you develop the qualities you need.

Money and Your Career

There is no point in your trying to economize, because poverty makes you miserable. Go for a job that pays really well and work your way to the top. If you find yourself temporarily short of money, take a part-time job in the catering field for a while.

Times of Change

There are times in your life when certain planets return to the position in the sky that they occupied when you were born. It is at the times of these returns that you will consider the need for change. The two returns that will influence success in your life are the first Saturn return when you are about 30 years of age, and the Uranus half-return when you are about 40.

Age 25–35

This Saturn return is likely to make you suddenly aware that you still have a lot to achieve in life. No matter how successful your business or private life, you may be feeling "Is this all there is?" Now is a good time to discuss your ideas with other people. If changes must be made, tackle them with confidence and ensure that you are progressing in the right direction.

Age 36–39

By the time of this Uranus half-return, you should be reaping the benefits of the decisions you made around your 30th birthday. On the other hand, you may have opted out 10 years ago and now be wishing that you acted differently. Do not despair. It is not too late to make changes that could lead to success beyond your wildest dreams. You are likely to reap the benefits of years of hard work at this time.

Age 57–60

You cannot wait to retire, because there are so many other interesting things for you to do. If you cannot afford to give up work altogether, you will downshift to a part-time occupation in some attractive and pleasant field of work.

Career Possibilities

1. Lawyer
2. Trade union negotiator
3. Marriage counselor
4. Legal secretary
5. Recruitment agent
6. Artist
7. Designer
8. Beautician
9. Makeup artist
10. Hair/nail artist
11. Massage therapist
12. Singer
13. Musician
14. Artist
15. Photographer
16. Interior decorator
17. House painter
18. Pilot

▶ *Do What You Love Doing*

However much you want to succeed, do not be tempted to take on work you dislike merely because you think it will make a lot of money or lead you into socially acceptable circles. A noisy or dirty environment is anathema to you, so you should avoid it even if the job pays megabucks. If you take the easy option and end up hating it, you will become stressed and unhappy—and then you will become ill. Success does not come that way.

It's easy for you to be carried away with enthusiasm for something new. You tend to become excited by a new challenge, but you may also gloss over the distasteful aspects. Don't allow this to happen. Within a very short time, those flaws will assume gigantic proportions. This particularly applies when you are looking for a partner.

Find ways to combine your likes and dislikes in order to find success. Though you enjoy good-tempered debate, you hate violence and injustice. The combination of these Libra traits could make you into a fine lawyer. A job as a personnel officer could successfully merge your diplomacy with your manipulative tendency. If you find it difficult to totally eliminate your negative traits, look for ways to use them in combination with your positive qualities. Your love of beauty could take you into the fashion or cosmetics industry. It is a fact that most beauticians, hairdressers, makeup artists, and the like are either born under your sign or the other Venus-ruled sign of Taurus. Music and singing appeal to you as well, so this could become at least a part-time career if not your main one.

Face it—you are not an innovator, though you enjoy developing other people's ideas. Try to find a business partner who is an ideas person. You will work well together and enjoy a successful partnership. If the ideas the two of you are developing require some aesthetic input, your artistic qualities will come to the fore.

Libra Health

If you are to be healthy and successful, you need a partner or a companion because working or living alone will be detrimental to your health. You need a confidant who is willing to give you moral support. More than any other sign of the zodiac, Libra craves attention and lots of tender loving care, particularly when you are ill. A tranquil home atmosphere is essential to your well-being. Without it, you will become stressed and eventually you will not be able to cope.

Physical problems are likely to be mainly associated with your lower back, kidneys, and bladder. Maintain a high liquid intake. Coffee is your favorite drink, but that can have some drawbacks so drink as much water as you can. Avoid an excess of alcohol, as this will harm your liver, which could be another weak spot.

Emotional problems will adversely affect your health, accentuating your fear of solitude. Push yourself into getting out and finding some congenial company—join a club or go to an evening class. At all costs, avoid staying home and indulging in comfort eating. Don't be tempted to use work to escape family problems. You will become exhausted, and then you will make mistakes that will take time and possibly money to rectify. Neither should you seek to restore your self-confidence by indulging in a clandestine affair. That is not your scene and you will end up feeling guilty.

Librans are apt to regard poor health as a sign of weakness, so you tend to ignore health problems until they become so bad you end up in the hospital. You will never be a hypochondriac, but you must learn to take reasonable care of yourself.

Libra Relationships

It is essential for you to have a partner who is your intellectual equal. This applies to both your private life and your career. You will never feel truly comfortable with anyone who is not on your wavelength. You need someone who will support you in your quest for success and who will urge you on to greater heights.

The ideal partner for Libra, in love or in business, is an Aquarian. You share the same tastes and interests and will be able to form a stable, lasting relationship. If you are feeling depressed, there is no one better than an Aquarian to provide the understanding and consolation you need. You may also be attracted to the fire signs of Aries, Leo, and Sagittarius, because they know how to enjoy life and thus lift your spirits. You have a marked tendency to be flirtatious and changeable. Remember this and do not be tempted to form an alliance with the first person that attracts you. Take your time. Allow your head to control your wayward heart and check out on all aspects of the relationship, whether it is in business or in love. Don't tie yourself down until you are absolutely confident that you have made the right choice.

Libra Positive and Negative Traits

You have a complex personality that can militate against your desire for a perfectly balanced life. This may mean that you will sometimes be beset by doubts as you tread the road to success. You should cultivate your positive qualities and, as far as possible, eradicate your negative ones. Better still, as suggested earlier in this section, you can attempt to modify your weaknesses and combine them with your strengths.

Take your first step toward success right now. Check out the following list of Libra positive and negative traits. Mark those that apply to you. Now start accentuating the positive and eliminating the negative.

Positive traits	Negative traits
Amenable	Careless
Artistic	Changeable
Attractive	Compromising
Calm	Flirtatious
Cooperative	Indecisive
Diplomatic	Indifferent
Forgiving	Insecure
Friendly	Manipulative
Graceful	Narcissistic
Idealistic	Overbearing
Peaceful	Slovenly
Sociable	Superficial
Sophisticated	Sycophantic
Tactful	Vain

Over to You

Before you can expect to achieve any measure of success, you will need to become more decisive. Remember—it is your life and it is up to you what you make of it. Act now and stop waiting for the right time, the exact situation or the perfect setup. The plain truth is you are scared. Admit it—then go ahead, because you have nothing to lose.

Reread the section headed "Your Plan of Action" and write down your first accomplishment. Then note what you want to achieve next—in big, black capital letters. Read it and repeat it frequently. Eventually it will come true.

8

SCORPIO

Main Characteristics

(Typically October 23 to November 21)

Scorpio is a fixed water sign, and how well these attributes describe your nature—still waters that run deep. You are an extremely intense person but also a cautious one, and you fear revealing your weaknesses. "What weaknesses?" you may ask. "Your imagined ones," is the answer. Like the rest of us, you do have flaws in your personality, but you seem to think that yours are something of which to be ashamed. On the surface you are bold and confident but the veneer is thin. You are strong willed—some would say obstinate—with fixed views about almost everything. Your powerful personality can be somewhat overwhelming, so you must take care not to intimidate others.

One Scorpio characteristic that will prove extremely useful to you is your penetrating, intuitive insight. You can sum others up at a glance, and you can see through charlatans almost before they have opened their mouths. The same ability is apparent when you look over a business document, even if it's on a subject with which you are not familiar. Nobody is likely to bamboozle you. Oddly enough, although you are interested in the occult and similar topics, you may be skeptical about astrology. Read on, and see what it can do for you.

Many Scorpios are excellent strategists, so you will not start out on the road to achievement without thinking things through and laying a few plans. You treat life a little like a chess game, working out how to go about things, while also considering what others are likely to do.

Scorpio usually has a distinctive appearance. Your most notable feature is your eyes. They are piercing, sometimes almost mystical and intense. Typically, you have dark, curly hair and thick eyebrows, a wide forehead and aquiline features. Being deep, dark, and mystical, you enhance these qualities with your clothes. Your wardrobe will probably include dramatic cloaks and robes as you favor long, sweeping lines. The darker hues of red and brown will always be your first choice.

THE SCORPIO PLAN FOR SUCCESS

Where are you now?

You may be reading this book because you realize that you need to make some progress in your life. As a fixed water sign, you can be rather like a still lake or static pond—in other words, going nowhere. You sometimes dig in your heels and refuse to budge. Why are you refusing to move ahead right now? Perhaps you need some exciting new venture to start you on your road to success.

New Beginnings

You are a determined person, happy to take the initiative, so cast aside any reservations that you may have and do it now. Remain astute and perceptive, but give yourself the chance to move onward and upward. This is the first step toward your new successful role in life.

Your ability to make quick and accurate judgments will stand you in good stead. This attribute will undoubtedly play a large part in your ultimate success. Keep in mind that we all have flaws and that Scorpio is no exception. It is hard for you to function if you focus on your flaws, because if you do so, your confidence drops away. You combat this by telling yourself and others that you know best in all things. This attitude makes it difficult for you to accept advice or to allow others to point out your negative characteristics. Recognize that minor flaws can be overcome, toned down, or even used to advantage.

One strange problem that holds many Scorpios back is your inability to negotiate in a reasonable manner, especially with those who you consider to be your superiors. You may use charm in order to win people over, or you may use aggression to keep them in their place. Scorpios are capable of both these tactics. You may back down too easily and then become angry with yourself for having done so. Alternatively you may decide to take a particular stance and then defend it to your dying breath, when yielding a little ground would have been more useful. Unfortunately, none of these tactics is much use in the long run—especially in the workplace. Work out what it is that you need, then negotiate for it coolly and calmly, and be prepared to gain some concessions, even if you do not get them all.

Just as water is able to change its shape and form, you find it easy to reinvent yourself if the occasion demands it. This ability will be invaluable as you tackle the life and personality changes that will be demanded by your search for success. Though you need to recognize and deal with your negative aspects, you must also develop and enhance your positive attributes. You are shrewd, dynamic, tenacious, and hard working when you get your teeth into something, so use these qualities to the full at every opportunity.

Once you embark on your new course of action, you are sufficiently resourceful to deal with any problems that arise. Remember, that commitment is one thing, while obsession is something else entirely—and it should be avoided.

Your Principles for Success

Whatever type of success you are aiming for, it is essential that you recognize a couple of basic principles. The first of these fundamental truths is that you should never try to achieve your success at the expense of others. Some Scorpios have a tendency to be jealous, domineering, and intolerant. Learn to control these negative qualities, because they will not endear you to other people.

You will not get anywhere if you are too self-effacing either, but it's better to err in that direction than to be overbearing and arrogant. You are likely to need help along the way, but you will not get it if people see you as bossy and officious. Instead, make the most of your compassionate streak. This will cost you nothing except perhaps a little time. It will ensure that you are seen as someone who merits success, rather than as a bullying tyrant. Inviting cooperation is more likely to get results than demanding obedience.

The second basic principle is that nobody is going to give you success on a plate. You will have to work for it. Few people will help you unless asked to do so—and as a Scorpio you may find asking for help difficult. You prefer to bulldoze your way ahead in the hope that all will eventually become clear. This may be due to your secretive nature, but you will find it quicker and easier to ask for help. There is nothing demeaning about seeking advice, and most people are flattered to be consulted.

▶ Set Goals

Before you can take your first step on the road to success you need to decide upon your destination and how you intend to reach it. In other words, what does the word *success* mean to you? Obviously, you would like to succeed in all areas of your life, but do not try to deal with more than one aspect at a time. Decide where your priorities lie.

Which ambition is most important to you? The answer is likely to be something that is significant because it is big—like making enough money to build a mansion. Smaller goals, like joining a classy tennis club, can probably be dealt with immediately. Achieving your main goal may well demand a minor revolution in your life—and possibly in the lives of those closest to you. It is a long-term aim that will eventually affect every area of your life.

Write down your precise objectives. Make this a succinct statement defining all the parameters of your success. How, where, and when will each point need to be addressed? Who else will be involved? Once you have answered these questions, you will have a much clearer idea of exactly where you want to go and how to get there. You may like to record this so that you can listen to it each night to reinforce your determination.

▶ Where to Start

Most Scorpios are extremely sociable, and you would hate to do the kind of job where you spend most of your time alone. If you must be alone for a period of days or weeks, you will keep in contact with your colleagues, associates, and friends by phoning them. You love shoptalk and gossiping about the job and the behavior of other people. Like all water signs, your mood can change when the tide goes out, and then you need to get away from others and to have some time and space for yourself. You need to find a job that offers you this kind of variety—some time spent with others and some time alone. For this reason, many Scorpios drive quite long distances, because the time spent in the car allows you to switch off from others and to think things through.

You can be changeable and suspicious and you can take your moods out on those who are in a less elevated position than you are. Realize here and now that a major part of your eventual success depends on getting along with these people. Decide here and now that you'll learn to become kinder and more socially adept. Make a determined effort to like people. Listen to what they have to say. If you agree with them, say so.

If you disagree, seek some area in which you have common ground. Then return to the point of dispute and try to resolve the situation together, even if this calls for compromise.

Above all keep your temper. Beware of becoming sarcastic and overbearing. Don't be rude and walk away simply because you haven't won the first round. Instead, say, "I see your point" (even if you do not). Then suggest approaching the argument from a different angle. Use all the diplomacy you can muster. Try what the television people call "noddies." When you are listening to the other person, nod your head occasionally, rather than shaking it all the time. It's a simple gesture, but body language counts.

Heated arguments never help anybody. Try stressing your positive points rather than denigrating your opponent's convictions. Whatever the outcome, finish with a smile and a handshake and if necessary, agree to differ.

▶ Your Plan of Action

Because you are an individual, the plans you make will be different from anyone else's. Although others may offer suggestions on how you might achieve your aim, in the last analysis the choice is yours and yours alone. Unfortunately, it is not possible to offer a series of precise instructions for you to tick off neatly until you reach your goal. Life is not like that. You must realize that, to some extent, you will be on your own.

This means that you will make mistakes. Be prepared for this. You do not have to be constantly apprehensive but do be ready to cope with occasional failures. This is no big deal. You simply need to be flexible. Regard every disappointment as a challenge. You will not always win, so resolve to learn from your mistakes. Try lateral thinking and brainstorm the problem. Be creative and if necessary improvise—but never give up. Like Thomas Edison you probably know "several thousand things that will not work."

▶ Getting It All in Focus

Second best is never going to be good enough for you. You have to win—and eventually, you will. At first, though, be content with success in small increments. You cannot have it all at once, so focus on one goal at a time. When you have achieved that, congratulate yourself but do not become complacent. Could you have done better? There is usually room for improvement, so think carefully before you take the next step.

There are no shortcuts to success. Don't be tempted to try them. Avoid speculation, too. You may enjoy the odd flutter on the horses, but be careful to keep gambling out of your business and family life because you do not have that kind of lucky streak.

Recognize your limitations for what they are—inborn natural traits. Your Scorpio tenacity and determination will help you to deal with them in a positive manner. If you are in a bad mood, work on your own until it passes, but do not be ashamed of it. You are not the only person to experience these "down" periods. Simply accept it and get on with the work at hand. Just one hint may help. If you can possibly bring yourself to smile, whistle, or even sing a happy song, the mood will pass more quickly.

Money and Your Career

You waver between being extremely tight-fisted and spending like a maniac, depending upon your moods. Try to save when you are in a saving mood and then you will have something in hand when the urge to splurge hits you. Fortunately, you are a hard and reliable worker, so you will always earn your way out of a corner.

Times of Change

There are times in your life when certain planets return to the position in the sky that they occupied when you were born. It is at the times of those returns that you will consider the need for changes.

The two returns that will influence success in your life are the first Saturn return when you are about 30 years of age, and the Uranus half-return when you are about 40.

Age 25–35

The first Saturn return is almost certain to provoke some decisive action in Scorpio. The realization that you are drifting through life will give you the determination to make some changes. Take a good look at what you have done in the past and consider what you feel capable of doing in the future. Think carefully—and you will realize that if you really buckle down to work, the sky is the limit.

Age 36–39

Providing you accepted the opportunities for change offered with the Saturn return, you should be in a satisfactory position now. However, the Uranus half-return could force you to question your relationships, your business affairs—and just about every other aspect of your life. This is no bad thing, but be careful to value what you have and to show your appreciation to the other people in your life.

Age 57–60

You are far too restless and energetic to give up work for good, even if you do not need the money. You may either find a way of staying on in your own job or you will look for something else. You are a good teacher, so you may take a less well-paid but more rewarding part- or full-time job in this line at this time.

Career Possibilities

1. Researcher
2. Police officer
3. Soldier

4. Fire fighter
5. Sailor
6. Intelligence officer
7. Engineer
8. Motor mechanic
9. Sales person
10. Travel agent
11. Physician
12. Surgeon
13. Nurse
14. Healer/therapist
15. Sports person
16. Sports trainer
17. Job trainer
18. Musician

▶ Do What You Love Doing

Ask any successful person if he enjoys his work and the answer will be a resounding "YES!" Obviously, then, you should follow this example and do what you love doing.

Give the matter some thought before you rush to change your job. A process of elimination may be the best way to begin. You like to be active, so you can immediately discount all sedentary occupations. In the same way, eliminate any positions that involve work that you know you will hate.

One of your greatest assets is your dynamic approach, so look for a job where your dynamism will be appreciated. Recognition of your efforts is important to you, though you dislike flattery.

You love to solve mysteries, so you may wish to become a detective—private or otherwise. Private detectives still have their niche. This is the type of meaningful work that you can get your teeth into, and that is important to you.

Don't ignore your hobbies when considering a new career. You are probably interested in cycling, driving, and flying. Apply that lateral thinking mentioned earlier. Design a better bike and you could make a fortune. Think, too, about any job connected in any way with driving or flying—there are dozens.

Scorpio often finds history fascinating—and yes, you could make a career out of that. Archaeology, archives, and unsolved mysteries all spring to mind. Why not go on an archeological dig to see if you enjoy it, or spend some time delving into local archives to find out if they fascinate you?

You may find the germ of an idea among the topics mentioned here. If not, then investigate more closely every aspect and offshoot of the things that you care for. Your perfect career, when you find it, may be one that you have never even thought of, but you will love every minute of it.

Scorpio Health

Generally speaking, Scorpio is a robust type that is not given to poor health. However, you cannot be happy or apply yourself to your work if you are not well, so good health is a prerequisite for success.

Although you are not exactly accident-prone, you tend to dash ahead in your eagerness to complete a job and this can make you clumsy. At times, your quick temper can also result in accidents, so try to keep calm and take your time.

The most vulnerable parts of your body are those associated with elimination and reproduction. Take care of your bowels and your bladder if you want to avoid problems such as hemorrhoids and bladder infections.

Unfortunately female Scorpios may suffer from menstrual and premenstrual problems. They are also sometimes prone to ovarian or uterine tumors. Many of these growths are benign but all should be investigated.

The body areas associated with most Scorpio ailments tend to be those that are usually not talked about. For this reason, embarrassment may tempt you to ignore symptoms or to try your hand at self-diagnosis. On no account should you do this. Anything amiss with your elimination or reproductive organs needs professional diagnosis and treatment—and the sooner the better.

The only other areas with which you may have problems are your nose and throat. Colds, sniffles and sneezes, and sore throats are all part and parcel of being a Scorpio. Fortunately none of these is life threatening and you will no doubt press on regardless.

Scorpio Relationships

For Scorpio, any kind of relationship is very special. Love is essential to you, and without it you will not be able to blossom. You are intensely emotional and for you a stable relationship is the only one possible.

Your ideal partner, for both your business and your private life, would be someone born under the sign of Pisces. Here you will find someone as intuitive as you are, who will be sensitive to your emotions, moods, and feelings. In your private life you will become deeply attached almost immediately and to a certain extent, you may become emotionally dependent on your partner. Pisces will be reliable and supportive at all times and a source of inspiration in your search for success. You will usually be completely faithful to each other, and this is important. Hell knows no fury like a Scorpio betrayed.

Jealousy can wreck any relationship. Guard against being possessive. Moreover, don't look for minor incidents that you translate as disloyalty. Be careful that these weaknesses do not drive your partner to distraction and end in separation. Success will mean nothing to you unless you have someone with whom to share your good fortune.

Scorpio Positive and Negative Traits

Don't be too shocked by the number of negative traits attributed to you. We all have them. You need to play them down and try to convert them to something useful. At the same time develop your positive traits fully. These are the ones that are going to help you. Even if you do not recognize them, they are still there, waiting to be built upon.

Check out the following list of positive and negative Scorpio traits. Mark those that apply to you. Now start accentuating the positive and eliminating the negative.

Positive traits	Negative traits
Compassionate	Cunning
Determined	Envious
Devoted	Intolerant
Dynamic	Jealous
Emotional	Moody
Forceful	Obstinate
Intense	Overbearing
Intimate	Possessive
Intuitive	Relentless
Loyal	Ruthless
Passionate	Sarcastic
Resourceful	Secretive
Shrewd	Suspicious
Tenacious	Unforgiving

Over to You

Now it's time to get down to work and implement all that you have learned here. Use your tenacity and your enthusiasm to the full. Few can beat you when it comes to intense concentration. This gives you an edge in whatever you decide to do and should keep you out there at the front, where you belong.

Carefully check your progress as you proceed and make any changes that will be necessary to keep yourself on track. Don't worry if you make mistakes, but be sure to learn from them. You will welcome the changes that are necessary in your life, and delight in the difference that they make. With your dynamic personality, success will breed success. Take your foot off the brake, put the pedal to the metal, and go for it!

9

SAGITTARIUS

Main Characteristics

(Typically November 22 to December 21)

Sagittarius is the mutable fire sign of the zodiac. Natives of this sign are adaptable and versatile—and forever restless. Enthusiastic, passionate, and impulsive, you are also generous and warm-hearted. These qualities will be invaluable to you in your search for success. In fact—you have no excuse for failing.

Even so, you need to proceed with caution. Your enthusiasm tends to be like the sparks from a fire—bright at first, but short-lived. Fire alters things and you enjoy frequent change. Those born under the sign of the Archer often suddenly decide to reinvent themselves and start a new life. This attitude will be a distinct advantage as you begin your search for success. At the same time, it will become a handicap if you keep changing from one path to another. Consistency and tenacity are virtues that you need to develop. Most people respond to your happy-go-lucky, friendly nature, but few realize that at times this may sometimes be no more than a cheerful façade. This does not mean that you are not honest. You simply prefer not to burden others with your problems. In other ways, you can be too open and blunt. Tact is not your middle name. Learn to think first and speak when you are sure of your facts.

With Sagittarius, there is a marked tendency for positive and negative traits to cancel each other out. This is something you should remember and try to avoid. For example, your honesty can make other people think you overcritical. In addition, if you allow your optimism to run away with you, you could seem unpredictable or opinionated. Try to take the middle way whenever possible.

You are probably above average height, usually large-boned and with a long, oval face. Your expressive eyes and good complexion are your best points. In later life you may tend to stoop and put on weight. Like the centaur, your body may have two halves that do not quite match, so this can make you top-heavy or pear shaped.

The simple, casual clothes you wear reflect your liking for sport. In view of your love of travel, you will prefer top-quality garments that pack well. Long, slender lines will complement your height, and your chosen colors are usually greens, deep blues, and purple.

THE SAGITTARIUS PLAN FOR SUCCESS

Where are you now?

It may be that your natural restlessness has prevented you from settling down. You believe that the grass is always greener on the other side. Well, perhaps, but when you are in another's pasture, you may realize it's not as verdant as you thought. Then you notice the next field, just a bit further on . . . and so Sagittarius is on the move again.

New Beginnings

Your constant restlessness may have some bearing on your current lack of success. Now is the time to take a closer look at a long-term plan. Be prepared to devote time and energy to making this plan work, concentrating on it to the exclusion of all else.

Right from the beginning, you must be aware of your positive and negative traits so that you can use them to the best advantage. Your positive aspects will be of tremendous value. In addition, sometimes—strange though it seems—you may find the negative traits, properly handled, as useful as the positive ones.

Your enthusiasm can become almost obsessive for a time. Then the fire cools and you abandon one task and move on to the next. Learn to pace yourself. Don't gallop ahead without first deciding where you are going and why.

Similar comments apply to your optimism. This certainly maintains a positive attitude, but you should guard against misplacing it. Sagittarius can be impulsive, rash, and gullible. You are so optimistic that it never even occurs to you that you could lose. Good luck, you claim, is just around the corner. All too often, that is where it remains.

Your Principles for Success

Don't be tempted to postpone your plans until "the time is right." There is no such thing—unless you are crossing a busy road. The only time any of us has is right now, so be prepared to progress, slowly but steadily, along your new path. Resist the temptation to charge ahead. You will swiftly tire yourself, so you may decide to take a break and that is when procrastination sets in.

In the beginning, try to limit your hopes. Aim for one small achievement per day. If you achieve it, then you will be elated and continue to work. If you expect ten triumphs a day and achieve only one, you'll be in despair and you will probably quit. In fact, the result is exactly the same, whatever your expectations—you have still clocked up one success.

You are a unique individual, so establish and make use of this quality. Devote some time to thinking about this. Clarify in your own mind what you alone can do. Then go ahead and do it. This individuality will set you apart from the crowd. It is the hallmark of success.

▶ Set Goals

If you set goals, even small ones, you are more likely to achieve success than if you have only a general idea of where you are going. Just be sure that your goals are realistic—not simply airy-fairy dreams. Your overall ambition should be divided into achievable targets. These can be subdivided even further into a clear blueprint of the progress you intend to make. Complete each small task before you attempt the next one.

Before you go to bed each night, write down a mission statement for the next day. You will then know exactly what you have to do to stay on course. Resolve to be disciplined. Set a deadline for each goal—and stick to it.

Inevitably, you will have setbacks. Ignore those that you can, and deal with the others as quickly as possible. Don't allow yourself to be distracted by trivialities. When something big crops up, take the phone off the hook and ignore knocks at the door. Focus your concentration on the way out of your difficulties. The more often you do this, the easier it becomes.

▶ Where to Start

In charting your course for success, realize that it will entail the sacrifice of a certain amount of personal freedom. Consider carefully whether or not you are prepared to do this. There can be no half measures. It's all or nothing. Listen to your intuition. Think about it and do not be tempted to make your usual hasty decision.

The first thing to do, once you have decided to aim for success, is to consider the changes you need to make. You need to organize your workspace, your life, and your mind. When you begin trying to modify your negative traits, then you have truly taken the first step.

Make a determined attempt to see yourself as others see you. Honesty is one of your strongest traits, so you are not likely to cheat. Are you all that you appear to be? What are you hiding? Everyone has a secret. What's yours? Is it something that is going to hold you back? If so, deal with it immediately. It is impossible for you, of all people, to live a lie or to pretend to be one thing while actually being another.

Tie up this idea with the decision you have reached about your future. Why do you want success? What do you mean by the word? Are you really heading in the right direction? Are you going about it the right way? Are you even thinking correctly? Self-analysis is not a Sagittarius habit, but it is one you should develop into a daily routine. When you check your appearance in the mirror every morning, assess your mental and emotional state, too. It will take just a few minutes but it will keep you on the right path.

▶ Your Plan of Action

Before you start on any sort of business venture, consider taking professional advice. This is especially true if the project involves teaming up with a partner. Do this for two reasons:

- ▶ It will prevent you from acting impulsively from misplaced optimism.

- ▶ It will slow you down a little, giving you time to double check every aspect of your proposed new venture.

A professional opinion, from someone who is not emotionally involved in the project, could be invaluable to you.

If you choose to work for someone else, do you know exactly how much you are going to be paid? That seems like a stupid question but there is a point to it, because you are better off working for a fixed salary. If you work on commission, you are bound to overestimate how much you can earn, which is yet another case of Sagittarian overoptimism.

Check your behavior. Are you argumentative and contradictory? These are habits that you must overcome. When you find yourself getting involved in a heated argument, STOP! Take a deep breath and, if you can, turn the argument into reasoned discussion. Words have power, so ensure that you use that power correctly.

Realize, however, that you cannot win every fight—verbal or otherwise. Develop your self-confidence to the point that, if necessary, you can simply walk away.

▶ Getting It All in Focus

At first, the overall plan for your success may appear a little fuzzy. Don't leave anything to chance in the hope that it will all work out. Get every aspect into focus. You have already decided on your goals. Now apply a little of the power of positive thinking and imagine that those goals have been achieved. You love a gamble, so trust your intuition and go for it, bearing in mind the need for common sense. This will give you the biggest adrenaline boost you can imagine.

Deliberately develop a burning desire to achieve success. Feed your enthusiasm and dare to dream. That dream will come true only if you have faith in it. Have faith, too, in your own ability to succeed. There is a difference between belief and faith. Belief is just a firm opinion. Faith is belief without logical proof. Until you actually succeed in reaching your goal, you cannot prove that your plan will work. You need to keep the faith.

Finally, develop your Sagittarius determination to succeed. Doggedly work your way through your plan, step by step. Ignore any jeers and criticism that come your way. Think through what has been said and make your own judgment. This, after all, is your life.

Money and Your Career

You prefer a fulfilling job over a high-paying one; as this may not be practical, you may end up doing two jobs. Your main job will probably be an ordinary one that takes you from place to place, while your other occupation could well be something that benefits other people.

Times of Change

There are times in your life when certain planets return to the position in the sky that they occupied when you were born. It is at the times of those returns that you will consider the need for change. The two returns that will influence success in your life are the first Saturn return when you are about 30 years of age, and the Uranus half-return when you are about 40.

Age 25–35

At this Saturn return you realize that you have been having a great life, but that you do not have much to show for it. With 30 looming on the horizon, you feel that it is time you started to put your many talents to good use. If you are reasonably happy with your present work, why not look around for ways in which you can expand it? If you are not happy with your job, take positive action and find another.

Age 36–39

The Uranus half-return is likely to make you realize (and be grateful for) the fact that you are a bit of a Peter Pan. You will never lose your sense of adventure, but by now you have probably settled down a little. If you are experiencing problems in any aspect of your life, bring them out into the open and talk them through. It is unlikely that you will need to make changes, but if you do, go ahead with confidence.

Age 57–60

If you can abandon your main job now, you will do so. This is the time when you might be able to turn your mind to spiritual matters or to a job that helps less advantaged people. If you are fit and able to travel, you may work in some field that takes you around the world now.

Career Possibilities

1. Broadcaster
2. Publisher
3. Teacher
4. Sports trainer
5. Sports person
6. Stunt person
7. Animal trainer
8. Minister of religion
9. Spiritual leader
10. Spiritual healer
11. Travel writer
12. Adventure travel leader
13. Travel agent
14. Scout leader
15. Lawyer
16. Comedian
17. Actor
18. Astrologer

▶ *Do What You Love Doing*

The counsel to do what you love doing may seem starry eyed. Nevertheless, you should at least try to apply this advice to your own situation. As an example, let's consider your love of travel. How can you earn a living from travel? Brainstorm the idea. If you write down the multitude of jobs connected with the travel industry, you will soon fill a page. You could be a cab driver or a chauffeur, work for an airline, on the railways, or on a cruise liner. You could be a traveling salesperson, a tour guide, or a courier. What about the entertainment industry? Actors and actresses are always whizzing around the world. In fact, almost any job you can think of can involve travel if that is what you want.

Thus far, we have explored the potential of only one of the things you love to do. Look at other interests that give you pleasure and see how you can unite them. For instance—you like gambling so why not work in a casino? You enjoy sports, so consider a career as a commentator, an athlete, a massage therapist, or a team manager. Your sense of humor could even lead you into a career in comedy. Your love of animals may direct you toward zoology, conservation, or training animals for film work. Think about these suggestions and, if they do not appeal, see what you can come up with. Sagittarius is never short of ideas. Your main problem is likely to be deciding which career you would most enjoy.

Sagittarius Health

You are not given to being unwell, but you are a pain in the neck to others when you are sick. Should you become seriously ill, your philosophical and positive convictions will speed your recovery. This is just as well because you may at times have to stay in bed. This is something you detest, because it inhibits your freedom.

You like taking risks and you do everything quickly so you can be prone to accidents. Anything from skiing through mountaineering to skydiving is for you. These are all hazardous sports that can result in quite severe injuries. Despite your love of sports, you can range from being somewhat uncoordinated to downright clumsy, and this can lead to accidents and consequent injuries.

Your weak spots are likely to be associated with your thighs and hips. These are the areas where excess weight will first appear and can be a good barometer of your overall health and fitness. Guard against developing problems by cutting down on the fatty foods you so much enjoy.

Advancing age may see you suffering from lumbago, sciatica, or rheumatism. You would be well advised later in life to eschew your normal strenuous activities and take up a gentle form of exercise. Walking is particularly beneficial to the hips and thighs, but do not try to do too much. Short, frequent outings will be far better for you than ten-mile hikes every weekend.

You are probably an animal lover having at least one pet. It's sad, therefore, that you may be allergic to them. This can result in asthma, when the only cure is to get rid of your beloved animal companion or find one that does not set you off.

Sagittarius Relationships

You may not feel that you need a partner, but you certainly enjoy having one—or more than one. Sagittarius is the most likely of the signs to have affairs. Flirting comes naturally to you and you enjoy a bit of excitement, but once the affair becomes boring, you will not hesitate to move on. In private life your best partner is another Sagittarian. You will both appreciate the other's need for freedom and neither of you will feel tied down. What's more, you will each be happy to allow the other to pursue his or her own interests. Life will not be a bed of roses, though. You will tend to squabble and your innate inclination to exaggerate will aggravate this. Nevertheless, in the end it will be kiss and make up time and you will be reunited, because basically you are both the forgiving type. A laid-back type of Aquarian might also suit you, as friendship within a relationship can be more important to them than absolute faithfulness.

For a business partner, you are better off looking for an Aries subject. Here you will find the stability and drive that you need to keep you heading in the right direction. You are both optimistic by nature, and this is always good for a business partnership. However, you both tend to indulge in heated arguments, and this can be detrimental to your relationship. Try to control this tendency, even if your partner doesn't. Bickering will get you nowhere, because you will be tackling the problem from vastly different viewpoints. You are fanatic about absolute honesty and your Aries partner cannot bear to be proved wrong.

Sagittarius Positive and Negative Traits

Despite your undoubted positive qualities, success does not usually come easily and this is partly due to your tendency to over-do everything. Your enthusiastic, adventurous spirit can easily tempt you into taking on too much at once. It is important that you should be aware of this and try to balance your strengths and your weaknesses.

Check out the following list of positive and negative Sagittarius traits. Mark those that apply to you. Now start accentuating the positive and eliminating the negative.

Positive traits	Negative traits
Adventurous	Argumentative
Benevolent	Blunt
Enthusiastic	Boastful
Expansive	Contentious
Generous	Fanatical
Honest	Impatient
Inspiring	Lascivious
Intellectual	Opinionated
Jovial	Overbearing
Optimistic	Overconfident
Philosophical	Overcritical
Sensual	Tactless
Sincere	Temperamental
Stimulating	Unpredictable

Over to You

Success will come your way only when you have learned to take the middle road. You have a tendency to see everything as black or white, and life is not like that. Control this trait and try to take a more measured view of every situation. Fanatics make life hard for themselves and for everybody else.

One positive quality you need to develop as soon as possible is persistence. Having drawn up your blueprint for the future, stay with it or you will achieve nothing. Realize that your private and business lives are closely related. If you are unfaithful in your private relationships, you will not be able to settle down to your career and this will put a strain on your work. Conversely, if you continually change your occupation, your private life will suffer. Loyalty and reliability are qualities that are essential to your success.

10

CAPRICORN

Main Characteristics

(Typically December 22 to January 20)

Capricorn, the sea goat, is a cardinal earth sign, so you tend to be down to earth, practical, and very cautious. A traditional type, you are probably an ardent conservationist who is passionate about preserving nature and wildlife. Your cardinal qualities produce high but realistic standards. You may not have a desire to rule the world, but you will certainly want to control your own destiny. You need a lifestyle that is fairly conventional but that is also financially secure. In fact, security in all its aspects is essential to Capricorn. Status is also important to you, and you are likely to take an active role in your community in order to achieve this.

Like the mountain goat, you will climb to the summit and leave behind those who are less resolute. Success, in whichever shape or form you desire it, is yours for the taking. Implement the guidelines given here and you will triumph in any sphere that you choose.

One of your most valuable attributes is that you have the stamina for the long haul. For you, neither quitting nor procrastinating is an option. Instead, you simply get on with the job at hand. So why are you not already successful? What's holding you back? It could be your pessimism. Before you can get fired up and take action, you need to have a clear-cut plan. Once you can see where you are going, you will be much happier and more confident. This, coupled with your overwhelming urge for success, makes you a sure winner.

However, one or two items on the minus side need to be addressed. You will sometimes have to acknowledge that your way of doing things is not necessarily the best—so do not be stubborn about it. Perfectionism is great, unless it becomes so obsessive that you are never satisfied. Others sometimes see you as being unpredictable and indecisive. In fact, this seeming indecision is usually associated with your cautious approach. You do everything thoroughly and at your own pace. You are not given to the fireworks and excitement of overnight success.

You will also have to judge which kind of Capricorn you are. Some are silent. They hang back, they hate making a show of themselves, and they hide behind louder, stronger people. Others are the exact opposite. They are talking machines who bore people to death and will not listen to what others are saying. The first type often does achieve success sooner or later. The second type starts out by appearing capable and confident, but then upsets the wrong people, bores those who matter by nonstop yakking or simply losing his way.

Capricorn is likely to have a sturdy build with piercing eyes set beneath a constantly furrowed brow. This worried look is exacerbated because you seldom smile. When you do, the corners of your mouth turn down rather than up. Your normal serious expression can be forbidding and this can make you appear sour or ill-tempered. Try the effect of the odd grin or chuckle from time to time. You have a lovely, dry sense of humor, so try to show it more often. The wonderful Capricorn golfer, Tiger Woods, is often castigated by the press for not smiling or playing to the crowd, but Capricorn concentrates on the job in hand and is too shy a sign to be able to be a clown.

You retain a youthful appearance well into middle age, and you are always at pains to appear elegant and dignified. The "little black dress" or a clerical gray suit exemplify your sober taste. Always conscious of the conventions, you dress faultlessly for any occasion. Dark browns, grays, or blacks are your favorite colors and they suit you well, but when combined with your self-effacing nature, they can make you fade into the background. An occasional flash of something brighter could lighten your serious demeanor.

THE CAPRICORN PLAN FOR SUCCESS

Where are you now?

As a hard worker, you have probably already clocked up a number of achievements—but something tells you that you can do better. Your innate high standards will help you in your search for the ultimate success. No matter how long it takes, you will get there in the end, simply because you have no hesitation in driving yourself. Be sensible about this. There are times when this urge to push ahead can result in exhaustion. Capricorn never rushes at anything, which is why success sometimes comes quite late in life. You can start in a lowly position in a small company, then slowly climb the ladder of success until you end up running the show.

New Beginnings

Given your overwhelming urge for success, it seems that nothing can stand in your way. So why are you consumed with worry, before you have even started to make changes? Could it be because you are afraid? The path you must follow is not a familiar road. To cautious Capricorn, taking the first step on to that thoroughfare is like jumping off a cliff. In reality, only your fears prevent you from flying. Admit this. Take a deep breath, then go ahead and make the leap.

What are you afraid of? Are you scared of making a mess of things and looking foolish? That possibility exists only in your mind. Others see you as well organized and courageous. Pause for a moment and consider—how many times in the past have you failed in your endeavors? The answer is probably hardly ever. How many of your undertakings have succeeded? Most, if not all. So, what are you worrying about?

Understand that your inborn caution and self-doubt could wreck this enterprise. You hang back because deep down you lack belief in yourself. This tendency to hesitate gives others the impression that you are being temperamental and negative. Accept, right now, that a positive and decisive attitude is absolutely essential to success.

Capricorn can be a fatalist. Avoid the "What will be, will be" trap and change your mantra to "Anyone can do anything." Recognize that you have negative tendencies, and set about overcoming them by changing them into positive attributes. Start with your pessimism. See the glass as half full rather than half empty. Look for the silver lining to every cloud. Above all, admit that your life is in your hands and you can do with it what you will.

Your Principles for Success

Make a point of focusing on your successes and not on the few occasions when you have failed. Of course failures are disappointing—but they happen to most of us at times. Analyze these disappointments to try to discover how you went wrong. What can you learn from them that will help with your future plans? Limit the time you spend on this analytical exercise. Once you have learned what you can from past events, put them firmly behind you and strike out boldly in the new direction.

Maintain a positive attitude. Make a determined effort not to sink into negativism or apathy. You may find this difficult, so try this exercise. Practice being positive and optimistic for just one hour a day, then for a whole day, and so on. This slow and steady approach comes naturally to you and will eventually become a habit. Consciously go about building up your optimism. It gets easier with time and practice.

There is no need to make huge, dramatic gestures to achieve success. Deal with your fears by taking small but calculated risks. In fact, making a definite decision to aim for success is the highest jump that you will need to make. Don't hang back on that decision, though, or you could miss a golden opportunity to change your life for the better.

▶ Set Goals

Chart your course. First identify what sort of success you are after. Be precise about this. There are many different definitions of success—wealth, fame, and power to name but a few. Aim initially to be successful in one field. When you have achieved that, you can start thinking about another.

Your first goal should be to deal with that critic who sits on your shoulder telling you that you are too young, too old, or too stupid to achieve anything worthwhile. This is your subconscious opponent who will denigrate your every move—if you permit it. Ignore this monkey chatter and get on with the job.

Concentrate on one goal at a time. You may want to keep a calendar on which you check off each small success you achieve. In this way, you will always be aware of your progress, and your self-confidence will increase as the days go by. Notice how each small success leads on to the next.

▶ Where to Start

Your first task is to deal with any resistance to change because this could delay your progress. You will be too busy worrying about "what if . . ." to recognize the stepping-stones leading to your goals.

Next, you must acknowledge your faults and shortcomings—your negative characteristics—and do something about them. When you see what's wrong, fix it.

Beware, too, of rationalizing your lack of progress. You are a master at self-justification, but this will not help you.

Don't take out your frustrations on other people. If you are feeling short-tempered, go for a walk and think things over. Don't spread your doom and gloom around. You will just make everybody else as sullen as you are.

Try to conceal your irritation if other people's ideas are chosen over yours. The plain truth is that those people may have training and experience superior to your own. Learn from them.

Capricorn seems to collect responsibilities. Now is the time to analyze each one. You will be surprised at how many of these so-called duties are in fact merely habits, sometimes brought about by an unnecessary sense of obligation. Decide first what you really want to do, and then see what matters and what can be dumped. You will then realize that many of your liabilities have arisen from the expectations of other people. Ditch them at once. You will enjoy much more free time in consequence.

If you are the talkative type, do something—anything—to curb the nonstop noise before others tune you out and put a stop to your ambitions.

One talent that you possess is that of spotting the right person in a position of authority to whom you can turn for support. This is a wonderful way forward. However, you must bear in mind that your patron might be moved out or moved sideways. Once you have been helped up the ladder, ensure that you can do the job well and succeed on your own merits.

▶ *Your Plan of Action*

Begin and end each day with a small ritual. When you wake, reiterate your intention to be positive.

Next, review what you did yesterday. Was it a success? How are you going to build on it today?

Determine to make this day special. How can you advance your progress to date? Decide on your main aim for the day, but do not let it end there. Are there any other minor goals you can fit into your schedule?

End the day in similar fashion by analyzing what you have done. If it has been a good day—sleep well. If you are dissatisfied with your progress, ask yourself why. Did you try to do too much? Could someone else have helped you? Perhaps you need to rework your ideas. Work out your plans for tomorrow and—again—sleep well.

▶ Getting It All in Focus

Having established the sort of organized routine that best suits Capricorn, you should ensure that you keep up with your competitors. Better still—get ahead of them. The more positive you become, the more inspired you will be. Carry a notebook with you and jot down any ideas or new concepts that come your way. You cannot afford to miss a trick. As part of your nightly assessment ritual, consider those notes and how they can be of value to you. With hindsight, you will wonder why you made some of them—but keep them anyway. Ideas that seem useless now could well trigger something valuable in the future. Allow your subconscious to work on them.

Be tough. That does not mean that you have to be looking for a fight all the time. In this context, it means taking risks, even though you would rather not. It means holding your tongue when you have to deal with fools. It means accepting with grace whatever life throws at you.

Money and Your Career

You will attempt to spend your working life in a secure job and if you have enough money left over after paying for the necessities of life, you will invest in property and also in stocks and shares. You are generous to your loved ones, so you will always keep something in reserve in case one of them needs your help.

Times of Change

There are times in your life when certain planets return to the position in the sky that they occupied when you were born. It is at the times of these returns that you will consider the need for change. The two returns that will influence success in your life are the first Saturn return when you are about 30 years of age, and the Uranus half-return when you are about 40.

Age 25–35

Your first Saturn return is likely to have a somewhat disruptive effect on your life. You may be fretting against various limitations that you are experiencing. Maybe you should stop banging your head against a brick wall and look for another more satisfactory way to get to the other side of your problems. Perhaps you have reached a crossroads in your life. Think carefully, take a positive approach, and step out boldly on a new path.

Age 36–39

By the time of your Uranus half-return you should have realized that positive action is more likely to produce results than worrying. Now is the time to take definite steps to ensure that your life is running the way you want it to. If you do not, you could end up a bitter and disappointed oldster. You can avoid that fate simply by broadening your horizons and taking a fresh look at life.

Age 57–60

Although you will be winding down from your hectic working life now, you are unlikely to give up work altogether. Indeed, there may be more career mountains for you to climb at this stage. However, you will want to spend time on active hobbies now and also to travel a little.

Career Possibilities

1. Banker
2. Accountant
3. Company director
4. Financial director
5. Office manger
6. Event organizer
7. Publisher
8. Editor
9. Statistician
10. Researcher
11. Gardener
12. Market gardener
13. Caterer
14. Caregiver for the elderly
15. Social worker
16. Wardrobe master
17 Teacher
18. Numismatist

▶ *Do What You Love Doing*

It's a fact that you will be more successful if you are doing something that you enjoy. Consider all the things you like to do. How many of these subjects could be used in building a new career? You have probably never considered your hobbies and interests in this light, so focus on these now. Most Capricorns love music in one form or another.

Perhaps you play an instrument. Could you study to become a concert soloist? If so, what is preventing you from doing so? Maybe you do not practice enough. Possibly you need a better teacher. Alternatively, is it that you simply lack the self-confidence? Many Capricorns are wonderful dancers. The precision that is required in music and dance steps comes easily to you, even though your movements will be a little stiff and jerky at first.

If you prefer to keep out of the spotlight, how about composing music? This is a solitary endeavor well suited to your temperament. If this doesn't appeal, how about teaching others to play your instrument? There are other possibilities. You could teach the theory of music, become an authority on the lives of the composers or, if you are a practical type, make musical instruments. You could become the top salesman in a music store. If pop music is your scene, consider setting up your own group or becoming a DJ.

All these suggestions are connected with music—just one of the things you enjoy. Now consider your other passions and see what you can come up with. Examine all the possibilities and don't dismiss any idea until you have explored it completely. For example, many of you love antiques and you are expert at learning and remembering silver hallmarks, the marks on china, and the details on pieces of furniture.

Capricorn Health

Capricorn children are sometimes a little delicate, but they usually outgrow their childish ailments and become more robust.

The source of most of your problems seems to be your bones, especially your knees. Ensure that you have a good intake of calcium to keep them healthy. Drink a lot of milk. Take as much regular exercise as you can fit into your day. Long hours spent at a desk will aggravate any knee problems and could eventually lead to arthritis. Take frequent breaks, stand up, and move around.

You should take particular care of your delicate skin. The use of creams and moisturizing lotions is almost essential. Too much sunlight is particularly hazardous for Capricorn, although a lack of it can also affect your skin. Go out into the sunshine by all means, but use a high factor sunscreen even when there are clouds in the sky. Your complexion is a good indicator of your general health. Learn to recognize its messages and use it as a barometer. For example, a mild rash or even light eczema may be caused by stress.

Another weak point in your system is your teeth. Take care of them. Bad teeth not only affect your appearance but they can also lead to illness.

Capricorn Relationships

You are probably emotionally insecure—hence your excessive caution, particularly in forming relationships. This insecurity can at times make you appear cold and distant or apt to start a relationship and then cut off when it begins to mean something to you. Capricorn feels it is essential to succeed in just about every endeavor. No matter what other people think, you need to prove to yourself that you are capable of achieving what you set out to do.

In your private life, you may not find a permanent partner for some years. This may be due to your emotional insecurity and caution or your drive to succeed in your professional aims before committing yourself to a long-term relationship. It may also be due to your inability to cut the apron strings between you and your parents.

A Virgo subject will be your perfect partner. You will discover that you are in total agreement about the more important things in life. Most of all you share the quality of common sense, as you are both earth signs. You will be totally compatible, able to laugh and weep together, sharing your inmost secrets. On the other hand, you will each be willing to give your partner the personal space he or she needs. This lively partnership will last, simply because you will never get bored with each other. Another successful partnership may be with a Scorpio. You are different in many ways but you share a fondness for family life and you both have intense feelings that you are unwilling to share with outsiders. You both fear loss and abandonment.

For a business partner, you would be better off considering someone with the star sign Taurus. Here you have someone solid, dependable, and totally trustworthy. Like you, Taurus is an earth sign, which keeps both feet firmly on the ground. Furthermore, you will share the same urge for success and enjoy working toward it. Together you should be invincible.

Capricorn Positive and Negative Traits

You should be aware of your weaknesses but, at the same time, acknowledge your many positive traits. Use those strengths to help you modify or overcome the negative characteristics that could militate against you.

Check out the lists of positive and negative Capricorn traits below. Mark those that apply to you. Now start accentuating the positive and eliminating the negative.

Positive traits	Negative traits
Ambitious	Calculating
Cautious	Dictatorial
Conventional	Domineering
Hardworking	Fatalistic
Organized	Indifferent
Patient	Inhibited
Persevering	Intolerant
Prudent	Miserly
Reserved	Pessimistic
Resourceful	Rigid
Responsible	Selfish
Scrupulous	Severe
Serious	Suspicious
Thoughtful	Unforgiving

Over to You

Thanks to your earth element, you will not waste time on abstract concepts. You are ambitious and certainly do not lack motivation. You will work hard to achieve your ambition and make a success of your life. Just be sure that you have a solid foundation on which to build—a written statement of intent that you know you can follow. Regard this plan as a contract into which you have entered. Use it to convert your ideas, your dreams, and your aspirations into something material. Once you have started on your mission, there will be no turning back. You will keep on to the end of the road and the success you are sure to achieve.

11

AQUARIUS

Main Characteristics

(Typically January 21 to February 18)

Aquarius, the water carrier, is the fixed air sign of the zodiac. You
have definite opinions about everything and are invariably convinced that you are right. Having reached a decision about a person
or a situation, you will not be moved and will go to great lengths to
convince others of the error of their ways. You need to learn that
there are two sides to a coin. You can be a somewhat complex character. Though you try to convince everybody that you know best
about everything, you can be strangely reluctant to explain your
views. This may be due to a deep-down lack of confidence. There
are times when, despite your apparent composure, you are unsure
of who you are, what you are doing, or why. As a result, others may
consider you perverse and eccentric.

Stability is essential to you in both your private and business
life. Aquarius is often perfectly happy to stay in the same job and
live in the same house indefinitely. This fixed attitude seldom sits
happily with the air element. You are an ideas person, never at a

loss for unusual and inspiring suggestions, but you need a practical partner who can bring you down to earth.

We are currently in the Aquarian age, so you should come into your own. All the omens are in your favor. What's more, you possess many strong, positive points that will help you in your search for success. To begin with, you are naturally talented and creative, with a clever mind. You make friends easily, and usually have a few intimates on whom you can rely. Much of your success could come from your flamboyant ideas. That is not to say that they are all brilliant. Only those close to you know how weird some of them are. However, the plus point here is that your ideas come thick and fast.

Because you tend to dig your heels in over everything, it's inevitable that you will experience failure. However, this does not worry you. If you fail, you will simply shrug it off and start again, probably pursuing a different theme.

Usually taller than average, Aquarius has attractive features, with a long neck and a determined chin. You often have a dreamy look, giving the impression that you are on Cloud Nine, conjuring up some strange new scheme. As becomes your eccentric personality, you like to be noticed. Ethnic styles appeal to you and you prefer vivid colors, particularly the blues. Others may deplore your taste but they will never consider you dull.

THE AQUARIUS PLAN FOR SUCCESS

Where are you now?

You lead such a full life that you have probably never thought seriously about where you are going. In any case, you see no point in worrying about the future and you are not interested in great wealth or in impressing others, although you like having money to spend on your hobbies or interests. You dislike being in a position of power or in the spotlight, and you lack self-confidence. Considering these facts, it becomes obvious why you are not tempted to go for the big time.

New Beginnings

If you do decide to branch out, it's essential that you find a project to which you can be totally committed. You need work in which your imagination and intuition are fully exploited.

In some ways, you will be happy to tackle new developments. However, you must realize that success does not come easily. You will have to give up on your need for constant variety. Accept the fact that success often entails long hours of work on what may at times be a boring project. You will find this difficult, but the results will make everything worthwhile.

This does not mean that you have to discard all your innovative and original ideas. You simply have to learn how to incorporate them into your plan for success. The bottom line is that you can change and you will do so if you want to achieve your goal.

Your Principles for Success

Apply the following precepts to every part of your success strategy.

► Try to adopt a positive attitude. This enables you to concentrate on the bright side and will help you in your dealings with others.

► Don't trust to luck that everything will come out right. This is not a get-rich-quick plan. Ensure you know about the less exciting aspects of success, like financial planning and management.

► Consider your ideas unemotionally and objectively. If this is difficult, get someone else to help you. Put aside the suggestions that will not work for you at this time, but keep a record of them for future use.

► Appreciate your own individuality. Few can match your creative and innovative skills, so make the most of them.

▶ Network whenever and wherever you can. Seek out successful people who can advise you. You will learn more from them than you will from books—that is, if you are willing to listen. Do try to adopt a more flexible attitude.

▶ Set Goals

Your next step must be to chart your course. It's impossible to plan your overall strategy in one fell swoop. Break it down into small, manageable units that you can see, understand, and believe in. If any one piece seems too complex, divide it further into smaller tasks. In this way, tackling one small aim at a time, you will enjoy the satisfaction of achievement more frequently.

The best way to set out your goals is in a loose-leaf binder or on index cards. Begin with just two pages or two cards. One represents where you are now, the other your final aim. Between these, in chronological order, record the steps you must take to reach your target. This system has the advantage that it allows you to break down the large steps into smaller ones, as above. Give one page or card to each goal and gradually construct your forward march.

▶ Where to Start

So far, you have decided on your goals and set them out. You will feel satisfied about this, but remember that these pages or cards represent only what you intend to do. We all know where good intentions lead, so let's look at what you can do right now. What immediate steps can you take to start on the road to success? Decide to use your many talents, but in a structured and practical way. We are talking matter-of-fact, mundane common sense here. Forget your lofty ideals. Above all, do not get caught up in one of your crazy dreams and start chasing rainbows. Be realistic. This is the only way that you can be certain of success.

Ensure that you have the time, the place, and the right mental attitude before you tackle these decisions. From now on you must look at every detail of every idea that occurs to you and ask yourself if this is going to contribute to your success. If the answer is yes, decide where it fits in and file it accordingly. However, if it does not fit into your current plans, don't discard it. Keep an idea book or file in which you record every scheme that pops into your head. Even the weird ones, suitably modified, may be useful at some future date.

▶ Your Plan of Action

Realize that you will have to work conscientiously and consistently. That does not mean that your life has to be all hustle, bustle, and stress. Use the K.I.S.S. theory—"Keep it simple, stupid." Reduce each task to the bare essentials. Cut out any extraneous elements. The simpler a process, the more likely it is to succeed.

At the same time, don't forget that if it ain't broke, there's no need to fix it. Tinkering is second nature to you, but you can waste an awful lot of time and energy fiddling with things that are better left alone.

You have a natural and healthy interest in other people. You like to know what makes them tick and how you can help them. Nevertheless, you need to accept that not everyone is like you. They are unique individuals, with their own methods for doing things, and may not share your way of thinking and seeing the world. Avoid the temptation to be judgmental and scathing. Instead, make an attempt to understand the other person's angle and why he acts as he does.

▶ Getting It All in Focus

Do you now have a clear idea of where you are going? Consider how far you have come to date: Are you confident about the plans you have made and the way they are working out? Or are you still unsure that success is something you can achieve?

In view of your caution and your lack of self-esteem, it's not surprising if you feel doubtful about your own abilities. There is a way to overcome this. We all know the saying "To feel enthusiastic, act enthusiastic." Let's change it slightly to "To be successful, act successful." This is what you must do. Behave, at all times, as if you were already the success you would like to be. At first you will need to act the part. This includes your voice, your manner, your attitude, and your body language.

If you like, you can choose a successful person as your role model. These people always seem confident and upbeat; they are well-dressed, well-mannered, and usually smiling. They seem constantly alert and even the way they walk reflects their self-confidence. This is how you must behave. The longer you act the part, the more you will believe in it—and if you believe it, others will, too. In addition, because they express their trust in you, you will begin to believe in yourself. And so it goes on. The end result is inevitable—SUCCESS.

Money and Your Career

You prefer a job that engages your mind but you usually manage to combine this with a pretty high income. Just as well, because you cannot resist spending money on clothes, gadgets, and anything else that catches your eye. You may be far too generous to others, so you must ensure that you have something put aside for those times when you overdo the giving.

Times of Change

There are times in your life when certain planets return to the position in the sky that they occupied when you were born. It is at the times of these returns that you will consider the need for change. The two returns that will influence success in your life are the first Saturn return when you are about 30 years of age and the Uranus half-return when you are about 40.

Age 25–35

This Saturn return is one that can cause limitations and disappointments, and you are likely to feel tense and depressed. Changes do not worry you, but at this time you need to realize that they will not occur overnight. In fact, it may be two years or more before you find the route that you want to follow. Try to forget the past and give your attention to the future. Be patient and wise, and it could be rosy.

Age 36–39

The Uranus half-return is likely to find you involved with charitable works and organizations. Aquarius is probably the most gregarious sign of the zodiac. Your love of companionship will stand you in good stead as your career progresses. Changes are unlikely, but if they become necessary, you will cope with your usual light-heartedness; just do not ignore the need for self-discipline.

Age 57–60

Your mind is too active for you to spend the rest of your life slumped in front of the television, so you will definitely find something to do. This may be paid work or it may be something that helps others, but it will probably end up taking up as much of your time as your "proper" job did.

Career Possibilities

1. Computer programmer
2. Computer whiz
3. Systems analyst
4. Radar expert
5. Scientist
6. Psychologist
7. Television producer
8. Set designer
9. Electrician
10. Carpenter
11. Builder
12. Engineer

13. Photographer
14. Writer
15. Dress designer
16. Astrologer
17. Politician
18. Journalist

▶ Do What You Love Doing

One of the big secrets of success is to do what you love doing. This may sound trite, but it's true. Do you keep a diary? Aquarius often does. The daily writing stint is one that usually appeals. Furthermore, have you ever thought of writing a book?

Why not? Read how-to-write books, attend an evening class, join a writers' group. You will soon learn how it is done. Analyze every story or article that you read. Then practice, practice, practice. If being an author is not the goal you have in mind, you can still use it as a sideline while you are pursuing your other aims.

All beginner writers are told to write about what they know. This means that you should write about what interests you. For you, the list is limitless. You can write about dancing, flying, politics, theater, or any of your other talents and interests. You cannot fail.

Even if the idea of becoming a writer leaves you cold, you can be successful in any of the other fields mentioned above. You are good at lateral thinking. Use this aptitude to see how you can use your interests to earn a living. This is certainly a multiple-choice affair, because you are talented in so many ways. Your imaginative streak could take you into public relations, advertising, filmmaking, speech writing—even politics. Your gregarious nature indicates that you are more likely to be successful in large organizations than in small groups.

Many Aquarians have an affinity with tools. For some this means being au fait with computers and office machinery, but many others enjoy carpentry, plumbing, electrical work, carpet fitting, and so on. This kind of work allows you to be self-employed and to set your own hours of work and the time off that you need. A friend of ours worked in a bank and at one point, she had to take charge of twelve self-employed craftsmen of this kind. Eleven of them were Aquarians and the twelfth had Aquarius as his rising sign. We were also intrigued when we read a book that had been written by a cat burglar. He, his partner in crime, and all his criminal friends were Aquarians. Another friend of ours knew an Aquarian bank robber! We do not advocate deciding upon a life of crime as your road to success, but it just shows how the quirky Aquarian nature can adapt itself.

You probably realize that a routine, repetitive job is not for you. Nevertheless, whatever work you choose, your tremendous inner strength will stand you in good stead.

Aquarius Health

Aquarius has a bad habit of missing out on sleep, fresh air, and exercise. As a result, your health may not be good, and if you are not healthy, you will not be happy. What's more, if you are not happy, you are unlikely to be successful—your grouchy side will show itself.

The most vulnerable parts of your body are the lower legs and the ankles. Varicose veins can be a problem. In addition, if you are overtired, your ankles are likely to be swollen and painful. Though you are not particularly prone to accidents, your lower legs are likely to be involved if they do happen. You do not go in much for exercise, but you will be the first to twist your ankle if you skate, go for a hike, or even if you dance too energetically.

Another source of a few problems could be your nerves. You tend to worry, often quite irrationally. This is probably an offshoot of your lack of confidence. Positive thought is an effective panacea.

Most Aquarians are affected by the weather, which never suits them. They grumble that it's too hot, too cold, too wet, or too dry. Even the light (or lack of it) can give them cause for complaint. Many Aquarians suffer from S.A.D. (Seasonal Affective Disorder), hating the long, dark days of winter and suffering because of them. Spend as much time as possible in the fresh air and natural light.

If you must remain indoors, work by an open window or consider installing daylight lamps.

Of all the Sun signs, Aquarius is most likely to come up with strange and obscure diseases, accidents, and infections. These ailments are not imaginary—you are no hypochondriac. Thankfully, they usually vanish as suddenly and mysteriously as they appear.

Because your brain is so active, you should try to give it a rest at times. Think about going on a retreat (not necessarily religious) or find yourself some sort of sanctuary or hideaway. These are widely advertised in a variety of magazines and newspapers. You may feel that this is not for you, but try it. You will come back totally refreshed and much more able to face up to the daily grind.

Aquarius Relationships

It is often difficult for Aquarius to find and keep the right partner. Long-term intimate relationships are not for you. Today, you may fall deeply in love. Tomorrow, you will be so much involved with your new mission in life that you have no time for personal affairs. In a couple of days' time you'll be planning gliding lessons—by which time your lover has probably taken off.

Obviously, you need to change. You cannot be a philanderer forever. Neither can you persist in your overbearing attitude. You need a partner who will understand and tolerate your eccentric ways. Be sure, though, that you find someone on the same intellectual level. Aquarius does not suffer fools gladly. It also helps if your partner enjoys travel as much as you do. Fortunately there is one star sign that fits the bill and that is Libra, probably the most well-balanced sign of the zodiac. You will not only communicate on an intellectual level, you will share a passion for literature, music, and the arts in general. The deep respect and trust between you will evolve with time into sincere devotion. Don't ever forget, though, that Aquarius does tend to have a roving eye. Indulge it at your peril. You may also click with Sagittarius. This is another sign whose values are more spiritual than material and you may share many interests. You certainly share a sense of the ridiculous. You both lack tact, so you should not be offended at the other person's occasional offhand remarks.

For a business partner, your best bet is Gemini, another air sign. You share a marked ability to understand each other, leaving the rest of the world dumbstruck and confused. It takes one eccentric genius to understand another.

Aquarius Positive and Negative Traits

Self-analysis and introspection do not come easily to you but you should attempt to understand yourself if you intend to set out on a new path. Check out the following list of positive and negative Aquarius traits. Mark those that apply to you. Now start accentuating the positive and eliminating the negative.

Positive traits	Negative traits
Caring	Aloof
Communicative	Antisocial
Cooperative	Contrary
Dependable	Eccentric
Friendly	Erratic
Gregarious	Hypocritical
Honest	Impersonal
Idealist	Intractable
Impartial	Irrational
Individualistic	Perverse
Intellectual	Sarcastic
Intuitive	Tactless
Inventive	Unpredictable
Thoughtful	Unreliable

Over to You

Once you can settle down to it, achieving success should not be difficult for you. However, settling down is the problem, isn't it? Right now, you have fixed your mind on reading this book. You are probably nodding your head and agreeing with all you read—but what will you be doing tomorrow? Reading a book on hang-gliding?

You are a natural-born pioneer. It is always the trailblazer who is successful—as long as he sticks to the trail. You may dream up a thousand brilliant projects, but they will not earn you a cent if they are not brought to a successful conclusion. Refuse to be sidetracked. Pursue one idea to fruition. Then, and only then, can you begin to work on another. Perseverance is the name of the game.

12

PISCES

Main Characteristics

(Typically February 19 to March 20)

Pisces, the twelfth sign of the zodiac, is a mutable water sign. Natives of mutable signs are always adaptable, which is a great advantage when changes need to be made. Unfortunately, though, you can sometimes be extremely gullible. As a water sign, you are likely to be ruled by your emotions, and this is something to guard against. Of all the signs, Pisces has the invaluable gift of being both loving and lovable.

The zodiac symbol for Pisces—two fish swimming closely together—shows your need for companionship. At the same time, because the fish are swimming in opposite directions, it indicates that you can suddenly swim away, leaving no trace. The idea of escaping from your current situation is never far from your mind. This is the hidden you, the self that you hide from the world. Pisces conceals this secret persona by being too talkative, holding the floor, and trying to seem indispensable. When your everyday life becomes dull or difficult, you escape to the fantasy universe of your dreams.

Pisces is often shorter than average and slightly stooped. The suppleness of youth often gives way to plumpness as the years move on. You probably have small hands and feet and a smooth complexion. Your large, softly expressive eyes are your best feature.

You are not a follower of fashion, though your appearance is important to you. Light colors, from cream to the sea shades of blue and green, are your choice. In this, as in every other aspect of your character, you are given to sudden changes. Clothes you adore one day may be sent to the thrift shop 24 hours later.

THE PISCES PLAN FOR SUCCESS

Where are you now?

If you are not already successful, then you are probably like most Pisces, drifting through your dream world, offering a shoulder for everyone to cry on. So many people bring you their troubles that at times you wonder how you are going to get any time for yourself. Don't spend your life aimlessly floating. You can rise to the surface with the best.

New Beginnings

You do have great potential for success. The trouble is that you are usually happy to drift along, just waiting for something to turn up. You need to change your ways, exert yourself, and swim up river, against the current if necessary.

Often, Pisces deliberately gives the impression of being dreamy and reluctant to grasp opportunities as they arise. As a result your associates have probably given up on you, not offering you promotion or more responsibility. This could be a sore point with you, but it's your own fault.

The time has come for you to cast off this unworldly image and show that you have talents that you intend to develop. This means dispensing with your bashful attitude and giving up your habit of self-sacrifice. Let people know that you are aiming for the top and they will have to deal with their own problems in the future. Your true friends will be delighted at your sudden show of independence and offer you all the support you need.

While you are at it, try to shed some of your other negative characteristics, and that means not being so trusting and gullible. Check everything out for yourself. Prove to your startled colleagues that you are not as helpless as they thought. You can be quite assertive if you try.

Your Principles for Success

The first thing you must do if you sincerely want success is to step out of your fantasy world and put your vivid imagination to practical use. Dreaming is one thing, but making an effort to realize those dreams is something else entirely.

Develop your creativity, because this is probably your greatest asset. Forget about lurking around in the bottom of the pool. Pop up to the surface and reach for the stars in the sky. You have a lively intelligence and can quickly develop any new skill you need in order to achieve your goals.

When it comes to practicalities, be as objective as you can. Keep your emotions under control and do not give reign to your self-pitying tendencies.

Like the fish, you are a slippery customer, finding it well-nigh impossible to admit that you are wrong. Sometimes, you will even employ subterfuge to hide your mistakes. Other people invariably see through this ploy and you really must do something about it. On your way to the top, you will need help from a lot of different people. Prove to them that they can rely on your integrity.

Pisces has a funny attitude toward money. You like money as much as the next person, but you will not go all out to make it. You prefer to work in an artistic, musical, creative, or spiritual arena than one that makes real money. Your values are far more spiritual than materialistic. You can be stingy and penny-pinching in small ways, unraveling pieces of string and hoarding elastic bands—then you can turn around and spend money like mad on something big. You give far too much of it away to your children and other family members and you may even bankrupt yourself in the process. You absolutely cannot cope with bookkeeping or statistical work. If you put on an event, you will have no idea of what came in and where it went. If your job or your life requires accurate figure work, find a trustworthy friend who can do this for you. You must obtain sound financial advice before you spend a cent. In this area, at least, put your trust in someone else.

Another problem that besets many Pisceans is a love of alcohol. Not all Pisceans drink heavily but a great many do find themselves addicted, so recognize this and get help if you need it.

▶ Set Goals

Before you can set your goals, you have to define them, and Pisces will find this difficult. Forget about castles in the sky and set your sights on reality—even if it's only a studio apartment to begin with. Indeed, for unworldly Pisces this may be all that you desire. Success for you may be an educational goal, caring for other people or even something in the spiritual sphere. It does not have to involve money. Decide on your target and do not be moved from it. Follow your powerful instincts and you will not go far wrong. "I do it my way" would be an excellent maxim for you.

Having decided where you want to go, you can map out a route for reaching your desired destination. This is going to be a walking trip, with many steps along the way. You will encounter nice, smooth roads; rough, uphill tracks; and maybe floods—though these will not deter our intrepid fish. Yes—Pisces can be surprisingly courageous when necessary, particularly if your eventual fulfillment will benefit other people.

Create your route to success now, dividing your journey into manageable steps. The smaller you can make these steps the better.

That way you will more easily complete them and feel a sense of achievement.

Don't try to commit all these goals to memory. Make a note of everything you can think of that will be useful to you on your journey. Why not work out a route on graph paper, so that you do not have to cover the same area more than once? Then decide on a timetable, so that you have a clear idea of when you intend to reach each goal. Please remember, however, this is for real. There is no room for fantasy here. Ensure that your timing is practical and perhaps you should build in a little leeway to allow for the unexpected.

Keep this map in a place where you will see it every day and do your best to stick with it. Even so, you are free to alter it at any time, if you feel that change is necessary.

▶ *Where to Start*

When you have set your goals, you are almost ready to go. Decide to do something about the three Is—idealism, ineffectiveness, and indecision. These negative traits are your natural heritage, but you would be better off without them. They could be big stumbling blocks. Instead, try reversing them and using them to your advantage. There is no need to sacrifice your high ideals, but be realistic about them; become effective and be decisive. Pisces is supremely adaptable. You can change if you really want to.

Be tenacious and, no matter how many mistakes you make, do not even think of quitting. Don't allow your blunders to bring on a severe attack of self-pity. Therein lies failure. Neither should you withdraw from the race if you have a slipup, scuttling into your dream world where all is well if left alone.

Use your time productively. Don't be so thrilled at accomplishing one goal that you take the rest of the day off. Beware, too, of allowing any one task to fill the time available. Work steadily and carefully. Do the best you can—anything less is not acceptable. Let your enthusiasm carry you on toward the success you seek.

▶ Your Plan of Action

It will not be easy for Pisces to decide to make a fresh start in life. This is partly due to your indecisive nature and partly to your neurotic fear of failure. You will certainly mull everything over for ages before you make up your mind to have a go—and even then, you will wonder how to set about it. You are probably too shy to ask anyone for advice, but you doubt that you really are capable of going it alone. Don't worry. That will not be necessary. On your road to success, you will obtain the expertise and support of quite a number of other people. Try to establish a network of reliable colleagues to form an enthusiastic team. Choose those who are smarter, quicker, stronger, and even more ambitious than you are. Build a winning team and you will build your own success.

▶ Getting It All in Focus

Now that you know where you are going, you simply need to get everything in focus. Look at all your positive points—your compassionate nature, your strong intuition, and your rich imagination—because those assets will help you on your way. Take every opportunity to develop your strengths and to use them. On no account should you ignore your negative traits or pretend that they do not exist. They may be subconscious or even dormant, but they could bring you down when you least expect it. Face the truth, admit your weaknesses, and set about dealing with them.

Remember that you have to take the initiative. No matter how capable the team you have created, you are the leader—the one responsible for making things happen. Oddly enough, Pisceans can be quite bossy, so you do have leadership qualities, even if they are not immediately obvious to you. Don't hang back—you could lose opportunities that way. On the other hand, do not be tempted to rush into any new commitments until you have considered how they will affect the other people in your life—your team, your friends, and your family. Discuss your ideas with them. If they are unhappy about the proposed changes or if they will be adversely affected, then something is wrong. Rethink the whole project to see what changes need to be made.

Money and Your Career

You cannot work in a mundane job because you need a creative outlet or something that helps others. This means that you rarely earn great money. This does not really matter to you because you can live on a small income. However, you carefully recycle every elastic band and postage stamp, so you can often save a fortune by saving money that others routinely waste.

Times of Change

There are times in your life when certain planets return to the position in the sky that they occupied when you were born. It is at the times of these returns that you will consider the need for change. The two returns that will influence success in your life are the first Saturn return when you are about 30 years of age and the Uranus half-return when you are about 40.

Age 25–35

If you have resisted the Pisces tendency to drift and have developed your creative gifts, you may already be successful. The first Saturn return may find you well known in your particular field—but also flat broke. Naturally, you will feel frustrated, so you need to take positive action. Results will take time to appear, but you must persist. Look around for a well-paid job, because Pisces is often beset by financial problems.

Age 36–39

Pisces people are the "carers" of the zodiac, so you are often heavily involved with charity and good works. Strangely, the natives of this sign also tend to be self-pitying. The period of the Uranus half-return could be a wonderful time for you, in all aspects of your life. Your family relationships should be thriving and careerwise you should be on the up and up. Have fun and relax for once because you deserve it!

Age 57–60

If you can retire, you will now do so, but you will hardly sit about doing nothing. You may start a market garden, an animal rescue center, or some kind of charity operation now. You could have far more fun during your busy retirement than you ever did when you were officially at work.

Career Possibilities

1. Shoe designer
2. Artist
3. Musician
4. Dancer
5. Actor
6. Writer
7. Sales person
8. Travel worker
9. Potter
10. Garden designer
11. Market gardener
12. Caterer
13. Bar manager
14. Nurse
15. Doctor
16. Alternative therapist
17. Spiritual healer
18. Psychic

▶ Do What You Love Doing

Being caring and compassionate are two of your strongest traits. This is why Pisces seldom pursues financial success—it would be a hollow victory. For you, success may simply mean achieving happiness, for yourself and for other people. That's fine and dandy, but you still need to earn a living.

Look for work that will fulfill your wish to be of service to others. Nowadays, there is a crying need for committed people to work in the caring professions—anything from nursing and caring for the elderly or for children, to welfare work and teaching the handicapped or working in a hospice. The scope is so vast that you may find it difficult to decide exactly what you want to do. Don't allow your Pisces emotions to take over. Avoid getting starry-eyed about caring for lovely little babies if the idea of changing a diaper disgusts you. Carefully consider all aspects of the work involved, your reactions to it, and your own likes and dislikes. There is nothing virtuous about taking on a job you hate simply because it's a worthy cause. Almost certainly you will want to work with people—but do you prefer infants, children, teenagers, adults, or geriatrics? If at all possible, try to spend a week or so working in the sort of setup to which you are most attracted. Get some first-hand knowledge before you commit yourself.

Before you reach a final decision, there is more to consider. What about your other talents—the creative arts, your love of the theatre, your interest in the mystical and mysterious, your passion for animals? If you can combine any of these interests with the caring side of your nature, you will have innumerable choices.

Do remember, though, that it is of primary importance for you to enjoy your work. Don't settle for less. If you do, you will be neither happy nor successful.

Pisces Health

For Pisces, happiness equates with health. If you are unhappy or stressed, your escape mechanism will snap into action and you will withdraw into your dream world. Any form of insecurity will affect you badly and could result in depression or even a full-blown nervous breakdown. If the pressure persists (and this may be anything from a mild family squabble to losing your home) you may resort to alcohol or even drugs as an escape route. That way lies disaster. You can be one of life's rescuers, taking on a drunken or ineffective partner in life. This will wear you down and make you sick. Look after your own needs before you become a martyr to those of others.

The physical areas most likely to present health problems for Pisces are the feet and toes. This may manifest as bunions, flat feet, weeping sores on the backs of the heels, corns, and chilblains. These symptoms often do not occur until later life, so get into the habit of taking care of your feet and you may avoid trouble. Foot massage or reflexology may relax you, helping to ease the nervous tensions mentioned above.

Walking is the best form of exercise for you. Nevertheless, you will not enjoy it if you are tottering along in stiletto heels or cheap plastic sandals that offer no support. Always invest in comfortable, well-fitting shoes. At home, walk in your bare feet whenever possible. Swimming, always popular with the sign of the fish, is an excellent form of exercise. Simply floating in the water, relaxing and stretching your limbs, is another first-rate way to reduce muscular and nervous tension.

Pisces Relationships

Pisces tends to fall in love too easily. Then, when you discover you have made a mistake, you either endure the situation or do a sudden disappearing act. Sometimes you hang in there from a sense of duty and at other times because you are reluctant to admit you were wrong. You hate anyone knowing too much about you. This secrecy, along with an occasional tendency toward intrigue, is a trait that militates against a successful personal relationship.

When it comes to a long-term love affair, try to set your heart on a Scorpio. Here we have someone as emotional and intuitive as you are, with the added dimension of sensitivity. You are so much on the same wavelength that you could become quite telepathic. Don't allow this empathy to degenerate into possessiveness. Realize, too, that you are both highly sensitive and easily hurt.

Some Pisceans find faithfulness hard to sustain, so be honest in your intentions before you get into a relationship—otherwise you may break someone else's heart.

As a business partner you will not do better than someone born under the sign of Cancer. Your instinctive understanding of each other makes for a harmonious and peaceful relationship. The fish and the crab are both water signs, equally affected by the moon. Remember this when decisions need to be made.

The fact that you have vastly differing views about money is a definite plus in this partnership. Pisces sees it as a necessary evil—not a helpful attitude in business. Your Cancer partner recognizes the value of money and has a real flair for finance. The two of you could form a terrific combination.

Pisces Positive and Negative Traits

Have you ever wondered why you feel the need to be reticent? No doubt it's caused by fear, fear that others will laugh at you or be angry with you. Why worry? Those same people will be jealous when you reach the top and they are still struggling. You have considered everything carefully, so go ahead with confidence.

Check out the following list of positive and negative Pisces traits. Mark those that apply to you. Now start accentuating the positive and eliminating the negative.

Positive traits	Negative traits
Adaptable	Deceptive
Caring	Depressive
Compassionate	Escapist
Creative	Gullible
Gentle	Idealist
Imaginative	Indecisive
Introspective	Neurotic
Intuitive	Secretive
Loving	Self-pitying
Mystical	Submissive
Secretive	Superstitious
Shy	Temperamental
Trusting	Unrealistic
Unworldly	Vague

Over to You

You now need to decide once and for all what you are going to do. Are you going to abandon your high-flying ideas and retreat into your dream world? That's fine, if it's what you really want. However, do you still have a vague suspicion that you really could hit the high spots if you tried? The decision must be yours, but pay attention to your intuition—it won't lead you astray.

The final point here concerns your tendency to secrecy. You do not have to shout from the hilltops that you are going to be a success, but neither should you try to achieve your goals surreptitiously. Secret successes are as common as hens' teeth. There is no need to make a fuss about it. Simply inform those people who need to know that you intend to make a few changes in your life and you would appreciate their support.

13

WHAT IS
THE RISING SIGN?

Your Sun sign represents your basic personality. For example, it would be hard to find a Cancerian who was not a caring parent or a Capricorn who was stupid about financial matters. The rising sign represents the influences that affected you during your childhood and youth. It shows parental attitudes and the kind of programming that you received at school, among your friends, and within the society that you lived in.

The way that you behave outside your home and familiar surroundings is often a direct reflection of what you learned in your youth about manners and correct behavior. It also reflects the survival techniques that you developed while you were young that so often spill over into adult behavior. This is the heart of the nature versus nurture argument. Nothing is completely cut and dried in astrology, but a good rule of thumb is that the Sun represents your basic nature, the Moon sign shows your inner, emotional nature, and the rising sign reflects your early circumstances and their influence on your attitude to work and also to the closely related subject of money.

Finding Your Rising Sign

Your Sun sign depends upon your date of birth, but the rising sign depends upon your date, time, and place of birth. A professional astrologer will have a computer program that will plot an exact degree of your rising sign and also an exact position of the many other features on your horoscope, provided you know accurately your time of birth. The following method will give a rule-of-thumb picture that should be good enough for our purposes. However, it is worth double-checking by reading the information for the sign you come up with and also the ones that lie before and after it. If there is a discrepancy, you will soon spot the one that fits.

The speedy rising sign finder

1. Look at the illustration at the bottom of this page. You will notice that it has the time of day arranged around the circle's perimeter. It looks like a clock, but it shows the whole 24-hour day in two-hour blocks.

2. Draw the astrological symbol that represents the Sun (a circle with a dot in the middle) in the segment that corresponds to your time of birth. (If you were born during Daylight Saving or British Summer time, deduct one hour from your birth time.) Our example shows someone born between 2:00 and 4:00 A.M.

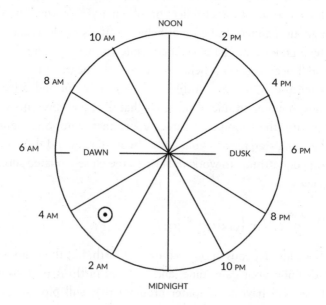

3. Now, place the name of your Sun sign, or the symbol for your Sun sign, on the line that represents the end of the two-hour block of time that your Sun falls into. Our example in the illustration on below shows a person who was born between 2:00 and 4:00 A.M. under the sign of Pisces, and the symbol for Pisces is inserted at the 4:00 A.M. position.

4. Either write in the names of the zodiac signs, or use the zodiac symbols in their correct order, around the chart in a counter-clockwise direction, going forward from the Sun sign that you have just noted down. Here are the signs in order: Aries, Taurus, Gemini, Cancer, Leo, Virgo, Libra, Scorpio, Sagittarius, Capricorn, Aquarius, and Pisces.

5. The sign that then appears on the left hand side of the design (6:00 A.M. position) is your rising sign. The example shows a person born with the Sun in Pisces and with Aquarius rising.

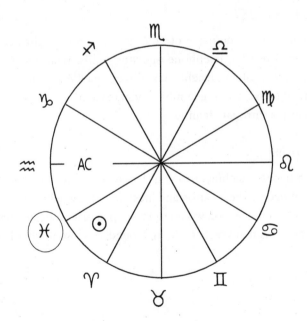

Careers and Your Rising Sign

The following will show how your rising sign might affect your attitudes about work and your choice of career.

Aries rising

This rising sign often reveals an attachment to and respect for the father, so you may take on his attitudes or follow in his footsteps. If this were not such a strong influence, you would look for a job in an area that serves the public, your local community, or your country.

Taurus rising

You learned early to value material things, so it is unlikely that you would go for a low-paid or low-status job. You may work in an area that produces goods and services where the appearance and presentation of the item is important, or you may improve the look of existing products.

Gemini rising

Communication is the name of your game, so you might become a writer, broadcaster, telephone operator, public relations worker, recruitment consultant, teacher, taxi driver, chauffeur, or bus driver. You may not have a loving family, so you make friends or work colleagues into a surrogate family.

Cancer rising

Due to a strong attachment to your family, your life and work may be determined by the location and lifestyle of those who are around you. Given a choice, you would run a shop, a real estate agency, or a small business that you can run in, around, or close to your home.

Leo rising

Your family expected great things from you, either boosting your esteem or damaging it by criticism—either way, putting pressure on you to succeed. You either become a great worldly success or you turn inward to explore artistic and creative interests.

Virgo rising

Whether by nature or by youthful training, your desire is to be of service to others. This may lead to a career in teaching or one of the caring professions, in addition to serving the needs of your family—perhaps also a charitable organization. You need to be appreciated.

Libra rising

Your talents lie in bringing people together and in providing a service that is of use to others, but you cannot stand being in a lowly job for long. Thus, you may opt for a career in the law or in some other field that brings status and money, but that also helps others.

Scorpio rising

Your upbringing taught you to be careful of what you say or what you do, so you might be drawn to work where confidentiality is important. You may look after the deepest and most important needs of others in some confidential field. You need to work in a field that matters to humanity.

Sagittarius rising

Your childhood was either very restricted or free and easy. You cannot be shackled now, so you may choose freelance work or your job will take you from place to place. You are a people person, so something that connects you to people and their needs will appeal.

Capricorn rising

Childhood experiences taught you that hard work, saving money and a careful attitude lead to success. This may take you into banking or into a large organization where you can slowly and steadily climb the ladder of success. You are ambitious for yourself and your family.

Aquarius rising

You probably received a wide-ranging education and varied influences in childhood. You are interested in new technology, new ideas, and anything that will ultimately help humanity. You may work in one field for several years and then take a complete change of direction.

Pisces rising

Early problems have left their mark on you and made you practical and capable, but you also have an artistic streak. A job that is unusual and artistic, but that includes status and an element of business will appeal. Among many possibilities are running a top health and beauty salon, putting on shows, or running an art gallery.